ENDORSEMENTS

"*Fellowship in the Spirit* is a volume long overdue. It has something for everyone, from the baby Christian to the seasoned saint. If you desire to walk in the deeper realms with God, then Spirit Fellowship is what you are looking for!"

Rev. Michael Plemmons
Virginia Beach, Virginia

"God's whole purpose from the start of time was that we walk in fellowship with him. He even sent His son Jesus to teach us how to do so. In these last days, God is still calling His children to fellowship. In this book, you will learn in detail how to do just that. I highly recommended *Fellowship in the Spirit* for people from every walk of life. It will stir up within you a hunger for a deeper relationship with God and encourage you as well!"

Iren Upendo Murrell
Executive Public Relations Director
Africa Transformation Embassy, Inc.

"*Fellowship in the Spirit* is an extraordinary insight into the realm of the spirit."

Rev. Richard Spangler
Lion's Voice Ministries, Chesapeake, Virginia

"It is not an accident to have personally known my friend Gene Markland, but a blessing, a gift from the good Lord and Master, Jesus, whom I serve. Likewise, it is my sincere conviction that Gene and I met through the miracle work of the good Lord. Since then, we have been good friends, particularly in the sharing of the business of the Lord. I must say that Gene is a

Books concerning divine spiritual things are inspiring, but as I read the initial draft of *Fellowship in the Spirit*, it touched the inner core of my heart. Many good books have been written on prayer and heavenly things, but I found *Fellowship in the Spirit* to be extremely real and personal. It answered the deep longing of my heart to know the Lord personally and have an intimate relationship and fellowship with him.

Fellowship in the Spirit is a book not to be missed for those who want to go deeper in relationship with the Lord. Learn to fellowship with God in the Spirit and your perspective of life and heaven will never be the same. Father in Heaven, Jesus, and the Holy Spirit are revealed as more real and personal than we have ever perceived. Finally, *Fellowship in the Spirit* makes the deep truths of the Bible so real that you crave the heavenly realm."

Joseph Lagilagi, Fiji

FELLOWSHIP
IN THE
SPIRIT

Angelic Encounters, Spiritual Warfare, and Effective Intercession are Waiting…

GENE MARKLAND

Fellowship in the Spirit

Angelic Encounters, Spiritual Warfare, and Effective Intercession are Waiting...

by

Gene Markland

© Copyright 2014–Gene Markland

All rights reserved. This book is protected by the copyright laws of the United States of America. Without prior written permission of the publisher, no portion of this book may be reproduced, stored in a retrieval system, or transmitted in any form or by any means—electronic, mechanical, photocopy, recording, scanning, or other—except for brief quotations for personal or group study, which is permitted and encouraged. Permission will be granted upon request. Unless otherwise identified, Scripture quotations are from THE HOLY BIBLE, NEW INTERNATIONAL VERSION®, NIV® Copyright © 1973, 1978, 1984 by Biblica, Inc.™ Used by permission. All rights reserved worldwide. Scripture quotations marked KJV are from the King James Version. All emphasis within Scripture quotations is the author's own.

DESTINY IMAGE® PUBLISHERS, INC.
P.O. Box 310, Shippensburg, PA 17257-0310
"Promoting Inspired Lives."

This book and all other Destiny Image and Destiny Image Fiction books are available at Christian bookstores and distributors worldwide.
Cover design by: Eileen Rockwell
For more information on foreign distributors, call 717-532-3040.
Or reach us on the Internet: www.destinyimage.com

ISBN 13 TP: 978-0-7684-0710-5
ISBN 13 EBook: 978-0-7684-0711-2

For Worldwide Distribution, Printed in the U.S.A.
1 2 3 4 5 6 / 17 16 15 14

DEDICATION

To my wife, Martha, and my daughter, Laura,
you are my heaven on earth.

Acknowledgments

A special thank you to all the teachers, pastors, and mentors who have shaped my spiritual life. Some have shared God's truths and mysteries in person, and some through books and other media. Though you are too many to name, each of you has a special place in my heart and I am forever grateful.

To my grandfather W.M. Arrowood, who from my earliest memory encouraged me to seek the face of God.

To all my brothers and sisters in the Lord, your fellowship is most precious. To my extended family, your struggles have not dampened your faith, and as always you have my love and prayers.

To my friends and co-workers at The Christian Broadcasting Network, especially those who proofread my manuscript and encouraged me in this work, I say thank you.

A special thank you to my Author Coach Keith Carroll and Editor Laura Barnwell.

To my daughter Laura who grew up during the writing of this book and encouraged me whenever I hit a slump—thank you, Sweetie.

And to my precious wife and ministry partner for more than 41 years, Martha, this journey could not have been possible without your undying love and support. Thank you, Honey.

Contents

Foreword 13
Introduction 15
1. Drawn by Hunger 19
2. The Timeless Realm of God 29
3. The Trinity of One 35
4. The Three Faces of God 47
5. The Mystery of the Gospel 59
6. Jesus in My Mirror 69
7. Effective Prayer 77
8. The Steps 87
9. Follow Boldly into Heaven 95
10. Heaven 107
11. The Beachcomber 117
12. Our Family Home 133
13. God Is Light 137
14. Angels 143
15. Angelic Encounters 153
16. Spiritual Warfare 159
17. Intercession 167
18. Church Fellowship 175
Notes 187

Foreword

Wow! Words cannot adequately describe the revelation that my brother Gene Markland shares with us in his book, *Fellowship in the Spirit*. Throughout history the Lord imparts knowledge and revelation through chosen individuals for the purpose of challenging the body of Christ to go deeper and higher than ever before. Gene is such a man. This book will not only challenge you, it will stir up within you a passion for relationship with the Lord, and then wonder of wonders, it will activate you to enter into your destiny of intimacy with the Father!

This is a season when all around planet Earth men and women are awakening to an understanding of their birthright as believers to both "see and go" into the realm of the Spirit. This book becomes a roadmap for those of like passion to enter into that realm with great expectancy. It reminds me of a child finally awakening to a Christmas morning with the anticipation of discovering what is in those colorful gifts sitting under the tree—and the sure knowledge that their dreams are about to come true. Prepare for the adventure of your life!

Bruce Allen
Still Waters International Ministries
Author of *Gazing into Glory*

INTRODUCTION

Before the fall of man, when Adam walked in fellowship with God in the Garden of Eden, he experienced God's glory with a spiritual connection. Adam was alive spiritually; his entire spirit, soul, and body functioned together as designed by God, on whom he was totally dependent. He had a perfect relationship with God and saw Him face to face. God in His vastness was just a breath away.

When Adam disobeyed God and fell, everything changed. He died spiritually and his connection to the Spirit realm of God was severed. With Adam's spiritual eyes now closed, he was left with a soul and a body of flesh. The glory was gone. Not only was Adam's ability to see into the Spirit realm gone, but the glory that had rested upon his physical body was gone as well.

Oh, that old serpent was right when he told Eve that their eyes would be opened to know good and evil, but his deceptive lie did not reveal to them that their spiritual eyes would be closed. The realm of God, yes, even God Himself was darkened to them. They left the presence of the glory of God and entered into a dark world of sin.

Up until then, Adam had lived a sinless life and was destined to live forever, as was his future offspring. However, just as God had warned, on the day Adam ate from the tree of the knowledge of good and evil, he died spiritually and so did all of humanity within him. He became a new creature, a beastly, sinful-natured being, and so did we, as we were all in him.

What Granddaddy Adam lost for himself, and all of us, was unfathomable. And for the rest of his life, he must have longed to have it back. What did he want back? He wanted to be as he was, and to walk in fellowship with his Father, our Father. Try as he might, even with all the sacrifices, he would not get it back. It would take a miracle. It would take a Savior. It would take the Word of God made flesh to dwell among us, and take upon Himself the blame, the shame, the sin, and the punishment.

The Lord Jesus did just that on Mount Calvary! He died and then rose from the grave, after leaving our sin behind in hell. He ascended back to heaven, and reconciled humanity to Father. Once we, with our free will, repent of our sins, accept Christ Jesus as our Savior, and invite Him into our hearts, we are born again into the Spirit, into the kingdom of God, and into God Himself! We are dead in sin no longer. Our spirits are alive unto God as Granddaddy Adam's was in the beginning. When our bodies die, we will live eternally with Him! Praise God!

But one little thing…yes we are born again, but our eyes are not open. As the apostle Paul wrote, *"we see through a glass darkly."*[1] In order to regain everything that Granddaddy Adam lost for himself and us in the Garden, we must regain our sight.

Our spiritual sight must be clear so that we might once again fellowship in the Spirit with our Father. In John 17:24, Jesus said, *"Father, I want those you have given me to be with me where I am, and to see my glory."* Jesus wants us to walk in the Spirit with Him and see!

Jesus promised immersion in His Holy Spirit. He told His disciples to wait for this Comforter. They received the baptism of the Holy Spirit and so can we! When we are born

Introduction

again and baptized in His Holy Spirit, we feel and sense His presence and receive the capability to see in the Spirit.

In Proverbs 29:18, it says that where there is no vision, the people perish. We must have our spiritual eyes opened so that we truly see the Lord! We need to regain the final portion of what Granddaddy Adam lost! We need spiritual fellowship with the Lord!

Apostle Paul felt so strongly about this that he wrote to the church at Ephesus, *"I keep asking that the God of our Lord Jesus Christ, the glorious Father, may give you the Spirit of wisdom and revelation, so that you may know him better. I pray that the eyes of your heart may be enlightened in order that you may know the hope to which he has called you...."*[2]

In this book you will see what fellowship in the Spirit is, and how God has restored this relationship with His children. God wants us to know Him personally, not just know about Him. He wants a face-to-face relationship with us. You are invited to see and experience what spiritual life in the presence of God can be.

The gift has been given, so let us receive it. God in His vastness is just a breath away. Our prayer is, *"Lord, open our spiritual eyes and let us see Your glory and fellowship in the Spirit with You."*

CHAPTER 1

DRAWN BY HUNGER

God wants you! From the earliest era of recorded history we hear the heartrending cries of a worried Father in distress, "Adam, where are you?" Father God sought His son in the Garden of Eden that day, for He knew Adam was in big trouble. He had fallen into sin. Father continues to call out to His sons and daughters to this very day. Why? Because He loves us, needs us, and wants us!

God has a hunger for fellowship with us. He has made it possible for us to have peace and fellowship with Him in the Spirit. God is not against us. He is our Father. He loves us.

Most Christians experience God in their earthly walk, but we can also experience God in the spiritual realm. We can be spiritual people as well as natural people at the same time. Being spiritual involves allowing God to be an interactive part of our daily life.

When we become born again, not only are our sins forgiven, but we are united in our spirit to Christ. We are born again in the Spirit; and God, in a sovereign act, places us in Christ. We are in Him and He is in God. So we are in God through Him. God also places Christ in us when we invite Him into our heart. So God is in us through Christ. This is why Christ said that no one comes to the Father except through Him.[1] It's a literal fact.

There comes a time in our Christian lives when we experience a deep hunger for God. I'm reminded of where it is written in the Bible, *"As the deer pants for streams of water, so my soul pants for you, my God. My soul thirsts for God, for the living God. When can I go and meet with God?"*[2] After many years of serving Him, I, like the writer in the Bible, was drawn by a hunger and thirst for God. So at Eastertime one year, I bought a new study Bible with the excitement and anticipation of going on a journey through the Bible.

Now I have read and studied the Bible all my life, but there is still something wonderful about getting a new Bible. There's nothing like the feel of the crisp new pages filled with truths yet to be explored, the new notes and commentary from a particular publisher…and the smell. Yes, the smell! There is an aroma of leather and ink that only comes from a Bible. Book lovers know this and savor it while it lasts, much like the "new car smell" that a car buyer enjoys.

It had been a long time since I had read, studied, and pondered the Bible purely for my own benefit. Sure, I had read and studied the Bible to prepare for lessons to teach, or sermons to preach, but a busy life had brought distraction from my time with the Lord in the Word. The apostle John wrote, *"In the beginning was the Word, and the Word was with God, and the Word was God."*[3]

The Word is a spiritual connection between God and us. In the same manner, our Lord and Savior Jesus Christ is the connection between God the Father and us, His children. So it is quite natural for my soul to hunger for the Lord in the Word, as the Word and the Lord Jesus are one.

I began a daily routine of study, prayer, and contemplation of the Bible, and my soul was fed. This new habit continued to be a blessing as days turned into weeks and weeks into months. I received the revelation of who I am in

Christ. Then, quite unexpectedly one day, the most remarkable event occurred. My eyes were opened into the Spirit realm of God, and I saw Father!

Apostle Paul wrote, *"Now to each one the manifestation of the Spirit is given for the common good."*[4] Little did I know that on that day, my thirst for God, the living God, would be satisfied beyond my wildest dream.

Here is how it happened. It was October 29, 1992, and I was praying in my office with my brother in the Lord. He told me that God had instructed him to pray for me, and that God wanted to open my spiritual eyes and show me something. Sitting behind my desk I agreed and said, "Let's do it."

He walked over and put his hand on my head and prayed, "God, show Gene what you'd have him to see. Open his spiritual eyes in the name of Jesus right now!" When he finished, I felt as if I were standing under a shower of gentle electricity. A force went through me from head to toe. This tingling sensation was the power of God.

Eventually, I opened my eyes and saw my friend sitting across my desk facing me. We looked at each other as we praised God with the power of the Holy Ghost presence upon us. We shared an expectancy of God's spiritual revelation coming to us.

Waves of God's Power

Waves of God's power washed over us. Praying with our eyes closed, our heads moved back as God's power rolled over us. When it subsided, we opened our eyes and waited for the next wave. Our spirits were energized by the power of God as this continued wave after wave. At one point, it became more difficult to see each other, even though we were less than five feet apart.

At first I thought my eyes were just teary, but then I

realized that there was something different happening. A fog, or mist, had entered the room. My friend and I could see each other, but only dimly through the cloudy mist. This was the holiness, the glory of God in the room. As we continued to wait on the Lord in the Spirit…I saw Him. I saw God, the Father!

Looking through the mist, straight across my desk at my friend, I could see from the right corner of my eye that Someone had come into the room. He walked slowly right between us and I couldn't move. I couldn't raise my eyes to see above His shoulders. I just saw His back. At the same time He entered the room, our surroundings changed. The room became dark. I couldn't see the walls, my desk, or even the door. I could see my friend across from me as Father walked between us, but our surroundings became dark, as black as space.

As He passed me I could see Him from the top of His shoulders down to His waist. He wore a dark purple robe that flowed with His movement. It shimmered with another color of light mixed in with the dark purple color. My eyes were fixed on His back as He passed between us and out of the room through the black space to my left. When I was able to speak, I told my friend, "I saw God. He just walked between us."

What a moment! The power of God upon us was so strong that our bodies felt heavy. We couldn't rise up from our chairs. It was as if our spirits were floating loose but the heaviness of our bodies held us down. I noticed the features of the room coming back into view; yet through vision in the Spirit I could still see God.

Sitting and looking straight ahead, I could see the room with my natural eyes, but with my spiritual eyes I was having a vision. It was like a television screen flashing before my eyes showing one scene after another. This is what I saw with my spiritual eyes.

God our Father walked out of my office, across the parking lot, and across the face of the earth. His royal robe flowed behind Him as He walked with His hands clasped behind His back. His strong posture and the slow, steady, deliberate gait of His walk showed Him to be the master of all that He surveyed.

He had walked through my office in the same manner. Now, through this open vision, I saw Him after He had left us, walking down a two-lane country road. He walked through a grocery store, then through a large department store like Wal-Mart. He then walked through an elementary school. Through all of this there were no people to be seen anywhere, just Father.

The vision continues as He walked down a street past an abortion clinic. He stayed on the outside and without stopping or pausing, just walked by. Next, He walked down the middle aisle of an empty church, out a side door and into the pastor's house next door. He walked right through the living room of the parsonage.

I could see the pastor sitting on his couch in the living room. The television in front of him was on, blaring away. A newspaper was laid open in his lap, as if he'd been reading it, then suddenly dropped it. As he sat there, Father walked right past in front of him through his living room. I believe the pastor saw or at least sensed the Lord's presence just as I was seeing it in the Spirit.

God walked out of the parsonage and into the White House in Washington, DC. Again, there were no people present as He walked alone through the middle corridor the entire length of the building, observing…looking. Next, God was in the Midwest walking through a farmer's field of wheat. The stalks were high; rising almost to His shoulders as He slowly walked through and surveyed this vast field that stretched out in all directions as far as I could see.

Immediately after this, I saw Him walking in various parts of the world. He was in the city of Brussels, Belgium, and then He walked the entire length of Canada. He made His way through Saudi Arabia and Israel. He walked down through South America and across the North Pole. All these images came very quickly, one after another. It was almost too much to take in.

God in New York City

Finally, I saw God the Father in New York City walking down Wall Street and past the New York Stock Exchange. Across from Wall Street is an old historic tavern that has been there for more than two hundred years. It's the place where George Washington said farewell to his officers after the Revolutionary War. I know the place because I have been there as a tourist, and during the open vision in the Spirit I saw God walking right by the place as He made His way down Wall Street.

I followed behind Him as He stopped in front of the twin towers of the World Trade Center. With His hands clasped firmly behind His back, He stood there looking up. Then, He was gone!

During this open vision, the power of God was upon me so strongly that I couldn't move. But when the vision was over, the physical heaviness subsided and things returned to normal.

At the time, I didn't understand the significance of Father showing up in person to see for Himself the places and things He chose to visit. I had no way of knowing, as He stood in front of the World Trade Center buildings, that just a few weeks later, in February 1993, they would be attacked with a bomb; and none will forget what happened on September 11,

2001.

Open Visions

For now though, I want to focus on the event of the vision itself. The presence of God was so powerful! Afterward as I stood outside my office and looked around at the trees and the sky, I could see the glory of God everywhere!

The Lord had opened my spiritual eyes! I had experienced what's called an open vision. It's like seeing two things at the same time. With your natural eyes, you see your surroundings in the natural realm; but at the same time, with the eyes of your spirit, you see in the spiritual realm what the Holy Spirit desires you to see.

During an open vision, you can close your eyes in prayer and see in the Spirit, or open your eyes. Concentration is usually better with your eyes closed, especially if the vision is intense and clear. But I have learned that you can have an open vision while driving your car down the road. This happens through the intuition faculty of your spirit. You just know. It's an act of faith. With your spiritual eyes open, your mind is aware of what your spirit is seeing.

The Holy Spirit can even lead you in the spirit throughout your day, coming in and out of the vision with clarity. It's just a matter of seeking the presence of the Lord and staying in His presence. This is how we *"pray continually"*[5] as the apostle Paul wrote, by walking in the Spirit.

This initial experience of seeing Father God in the Spirit satisfied my hunger and thirst for Him. How do I know this was Father? I know that I know. Over the years there have in fact, been many more visions and visitations, as I'll describe later. But I want to stress that you can have the privilege and gift of seeing in the Spirit as well, and it doesn't have to be a fantastic one-time event. No, the Lord has something even better than a one-time experience for His children. He wants walking in the Spirit with visions and dreams to be a lifestyle, your lifestyle!

This gift is not just for God's children of yesterday; it's also for His children of today! God spoke through the prophet Joel and told of this day, *"I will pour out my Spirit on all people, your sons and daughters will prophesy, your old men will dream dreams, your young men will see visions. Even on my servants, both men and women, I will pour out my Spirit in those days. I will show wonders in the heavens and on the earth...."*[6]

So friend, don't believe that this gift is only for the saints of yesterday, or for some select few. It is simply not true. Don't let that old serpent, the devil, lie, deceive, and do to you what he did to the parents of mankind, Adam and Eve. Christ paid the ultimate price to get us back, and to open the realm of God to us in the Spirit. Seek the Lord with a hungry heart. Seek His face and He will call you to fellowship in the Spirit with Him. This is His desire!

When we pray, we imagine we are before the throne of God. But what some people don't realize is that in the Spirit as we pray, our spirit is actually before the throne of God. With our spiritual eyes opened, we can see to whom we are praying!

During an open vision, with your natural eyes you might see the natural trees on earth, but with your spiritual eyes you can see the trees in heaven at the same time. People have written about visions of heaven and we tend to think that these are special people, chosen of God specifically to have visions. You might think, *That could never happen to me.* But I submit that this ability is available to every Christian! Any Christian can have a unique relationship with the Lord, entering into the spiritual realm and walking in the Spirit. It enriches our lives and builds our faith.

Apostle Paul admonished the church based upon what he saw in the Spirit. Someone can have a vision here and there, but another can also have a lifestyle of visions from the Lord. Now if you don't have a vision every day, that's all right. There's nothing wrong with not seeing, but the fact is that it is His will for us to see. All we have to do is ask.

Experiencing Life in His Presence

I wrote this book to share what it feels like, what it looks like, and how to go about experiencing life in the presence of God.

I pray the Lord will produce a hunger in you for a relationship with God, one of walking in the Spirit with Him. That God will open your spiritual eyes so you can see what He wants you to see and follow Him closely in the spiritual realm. I will show from my experience how God does it, what you can expect, and examples of things that you may experience when you do. This book not only explains walking in the Spirit, but the process you go through when you do. It is a life-changing process with eternal rewards.

The Lord wants all His children to walk in the Spirit, see His face, and fellowship with Him. You can prepare yourself to see, and allow the Holy Spirit to purge any trace of sin from your life. You can sanctify every faculty of your spirit, soul, and body from anything that might block you from having clear communication with the Lord.

Do you desire a closer relationship with God, but feel stuck as a mere spectator in church, an unworthy spectator in the faith? Does your heart desire to participate in the faith, experiencing the spiritual realm with the Lord?

The Gospels teach us that Jesus loves to experience people on a one-on-one basis. It doesn't matter who you are, and that's what I want to share. With God all things are possible. We have to believe that He is, in order to have faith in Him. We have to believe that a relationship with Him in the Spirit is possible, in order to have one. Search the Scriptures, such as the words of Jesus recorded in John chapter 17, or in the writings of Paul. The proof is there! Jesus wants us to walk in the Spirit. There are dozens of Scriptures throughout the Bible to explore for confirmation.

Just ask Him for that type of relationship. Seek Him and you'll find that the sky is the limit. If He will bless me, a fallible man, with a relationship in the Spirit, He'll do it for you as well. You might feel unworthy, the least of the brethren, but you can still have that relationship. Through Christ we can be more than observers. We can be participants!

The New Testament experience is for any believer today. This dream is possible for those who hunger for it. Sometimes you may have a vision that is as vivid as watching a movie. At other times you might be sitting quietly with God in silence, just knowing His presence is with you. Then there are events in your everyday life that cause you to seek the Lord for His guidance. Any subject that comes to mind, you may share with the Lord.

Heaven can be experienced now, as we live in two different realms, or two different lives, through our spirit. You can be physically in one place, and your spirit can experience an entirely different place. Like in a vision, here but not only here. We can be in a far-away time, or timeless place, experiencing things in visions, like seeing a television program and getting lost in the story. Yet we are actually lost in Christ, in God.

Chapter 2

The Timeless Realm of God

Time Travel

Have you ever seen a movie or read a book about time travel? Have you ever thought about going back in time to some of the great moments of history, or forward in time into the future? It is fun to think about. I would love to see great events in U.S. history such as the signing of the Declaration of Independence or Lincoln's Gettysburg Address; and biblical events such as the parting of the Red Sea and the Sermon on the Mount.

What fun it would be to travel into the future and see our families and descendants with all of their accomplishments. Yes, time travel would be fun and exciting. But if we could travel back in time, wouldn't we want to change some of the mistakes and stupid things we've done? Aren't there sins that we would not commit? Wouldn't we go forward in time to see the sins, mistakes, and pitfall that were ahead so we could prevent them?

If we let our imaginations go, the possibilities are unlimited. Well, with God, all things are possible.[1]

One day while traveling on vacation, I was in a bookstore perusing the discount table when I came across a rather small, hardback book by Albert Einstein titled *The*

Theory of Relativity. I picked it up and then put it down; then at the urging of the Holy Spirit, picked it up again. I thought to myself, *How could I possibly understand this scientific book written by one of the greatest minds of all time?* However, on the cover of the book, it stated that anybody with a high school education could understand it. So I accepted the cover's challenge and the direction of the Holy Spirit, and purchased it.

As I read the book, I found myself having to really concentrate on what Einstein was teaching. I had to go back and re-read until I got it, then go forward to the next principle until I accomplished my understanding of relativity. I'll never be a scientist, but I do grasp his concept.

Albert Einstein's theory of relativity proves that movement in time is relative to position. The Lord explained to me that I needed this concept to understand His existence in and over time.

God's Mastery Over Time

Imagine yourself in a car on a highway that runs from the East Coast of the United States to the West Coast. You are at one point on the highway, traveling west. There is a giant cloud above the highway that stretches from the East Coast to the West Coast covering the entire highway.

The highway represents time. The car represents your travel through your life on the highway of time, and the cloud represents God. You only exist on one point on the highway, but God exists over all points on the highway of time from the beginning to the end. He exists in the past, present, and future at the same time! As the cloud is above the highway, God is above and beyond time. He created everything in the universe that makes time possible.

God doesn't look at videotape or some replay of past events. He doesn't have to because He exists and lives in the past right now and always will. He doesn't look into some device to see a forecast of the future; He exists and lives in the future right now and always will! Later, you'll learn how prophets like the apostle John saw into the future that he wrote about in the book of Revelation, and how Moses saw the past in order to write in the book of Genesis, things that happened well before his birth. In God all things are possible!

Everlasting

In addition to God existing in all of time at once, He exists in everlasting time. Think about this. God exists beyond time, beyond past time, and beyond future time, simultaneously! The Hebrew word for everlasting is *owlam,* which means the vanishing point, eternity perpetual at any time without end. The Greek word is *ainois,* which means perpetual of past and future time.

The Bible says, *"Praise be to the Lord, the God of Israel, from everlasting to everlasting."*[2] *"Your throne was established long ago; you are from all eternity."*[3] The Bible says in Hebrews, *"Your throne, O God, will last for ever and ever."*[4] And, *"Jesus Christ is the same yesterday and today and forever."*[5] So from the Scriptures we understand that God exists at all points in time—and from everlasting to everlasting at the same time!

I Am

How can this be? Because He is the great I Am! God said to Moses, *"I Am who I Am. This is what you are to say to the Israelites: 'I AM has sent me to you.'"*[6] Who is I Am? The Hebrew word *hayah* means to exist, the self-existent one.

Looking further into the Word of God we see, *"In the beginning was the Word, and the Word was with God, and the Word was God. He was with God in the beginning."*[7]

Jesus is called the Word of God who has always been

with God forever since the beginning. Jesus said, *"I am the Alpha and the Omega, the First and the Last, the Beginning and the End."*[8] We read in the Gospel of John where Jesus said, *"I tell you the truth," Jesus answered, "before Abraham was born, I am!"*[9] He was saying that He currently exists back in time before Abraham was born!

God, the Father, Son, and Holy Ghost exist in the past, present, and future at the same time. They exist together and separately. Later we'll explore the Trinity and see how they are three and one.

Forgiveness

This same everlasting God forgives us our sins. John wrote, *"If we confess our sins, he is faithful and just and will forgive us our sins and purify us from all unrighteousness."*[10] This is such a wonderful promise! As we dig deep in the study of the Scriptures, we find the Hebrew word for forgive is *kaphar,* which means to cover, cancel, and purge.

When God forgives and cleanses us from our sins, they are purged from the past. They are not there any longer. It is as if they were never there. The sins are purged from time. Now here's the kicker. God still exists in the past when and where our sins happened. If our sins were still there and not purged, then He would see them because He is still there! So in order for God not to see them, they are purged and cast away!

Life Equals Time

Learning who God is and how He thinks is a challenge and a life goal. The more you study the Bible, of course the more you know; but the more you pray, particularly when you pray in the Spirit, the closer you get to them, the three who make up I Am. The benefits to us are limitless, and a close relationship with them—Father, Lord Jesus, and the Holy Spirit—is most precious. You can grow to a place in the Lord where you feel so blessed, so rich spiritually, that the things of earth literally pale in comparison.

When we accept Jesus as our Savior and become born again in the Spirit, we receive life eternal and life exceptional. This is the good part. The Bible says, *"What is your life? You are a mist that appears for a little while and then vanishes."*[11] The Greek word for life is *zoë* and it means life or time.

When the Holy Spirit showed me this deeper meaning, He led me to read certain Scriptures and substitute the word time in place of the word life. In order to fully illustrate this deeper meaning, let's look at some familiar Scriptures and replace the word life with the word time.

> *For God so loved the world that he gave his one and only Son, that whoever believes in him shall not perish but have eternal life [time].*[12]
>
> *I tell you the truth, he who believes has everlasting life [time].*[13]
>
> *I have come that they may have life [time], and have it to the full.*[14]

In Christ we have everlasting life (time) with God. We are in Christ. Therefore we are in "I Am" from everlasting to everlasting.

Martha and I were married for nineteen years before we were blessed with our daughter, Laura. The joy of that event has never faded for us. We remember all too well, the years of being childless, holding on to God for a miracle. As our daughter grew, the realization hit Martha that our little baby was growing up and in a few short years she'd be an adult and gone, leaving us alone again. Her joy became dampened by the dread of losing her baby in the future.

Finally she took her distress to the Lord and He spoke to her heart and said, "That's what eternity is for." The Lord reassured her that even though this life passes quickly, look ahead to the soon coming day when we'll all be in heaven together with the Lord, and our loved ones, for time everlasting. We are to comfort one another with these words.

Time Travel in God

Jesus prayed, *"Father, I want those you have given me to be with me where I am, and to see my glory, the glory you have given me because you loved me before the creation of the world."*[15]

As we are caught up in the Spirit in Christ, we are able to see His glory; and as the Spirit leads, we are allowed to see His glory in the past, present, and future at their discretion. In the Spirit, in God, we are able to see the past through their eyes, not as a replay, but since they exist in the past now, we see it as it happens. And in the Spirit, in God, we are able to see into the future, not as a prediction portrayed, but again, since they exist in the future right now, we see, through their eyes, the future as it happens.

Jesus promised, *"But when he, the Spirit of truth, comes, he will guide you into all truth…and he will tell you what is yet to come. He will bring glory to me by taking from what is mine and making it known to you."*[16]

So then, since the past, present, future, and all contained therein belong to God, the Spirit is free to show any of it to us at Their discretion. Do not limit yourself as to what the Lord will show you in the Spirit. God loves you as much as He loved any prophet of old. Seek Him, seek Them, in the Spirit, and you shall find Them. They'll find you.

Ask the Lord to open your spiritual eyes and take you through time and eternity to the place He wants you to see. There are realms of heaven and earth—past, present, and future. In Christ, through the Holy Spirit, we can travel in prayer to wherever and whenever God wants us to be. With Him all things are possible.

Chapter 3

The Trinity of One

To try to explain the Trinity of God is for many reasons a daunting task. Obviously, God is so complex and beyond the mind of man that we can barely comprehend His existence… Their existence. But He does reveal Himself and the fullness of the Trinity to us in the Bible and in the Spirit realm in which He dwells.

But for me, the challenge in discussing the Trinity is more personal; for as we develop an intimate relationship with the Father, Lord Jesus, and the Holy Spirit, we also gain insight into their relationship with each other. They allow this insight and want every child of God to have an understanding of Their relationship.

Their relationship is so personal, sacred, and holy that I want to be careful what I say and how I say it. Man must not be so arrogant as to think that God can be analyzed like a science project. On the contrary, we must look at Them with love and awe, as a baby looks into his or her parent's eyes. So with this as a guideline, let's begin.

The apostle John wrote, *"For there are three that bear record in heaven, the Father, the Word, and the Holy Ghost* [Spirit]: *and these three are one"*[1] So God is actually three separate personalities, yet one. Through Christ we are one with God.

The Mystery

How can God be three separate beings yet also one being? This doesn't make sense in our realm of natural thinking. Some say that this is a contradiction and actually proves a fallacy in the Bible. Some say that it's just a mystery of God, accept it and don't try to figure it out. However, when we hunger in our hearts to know God better, He will satisfy that hunger. What most people don't realize is that God also has a hunger. He has a hunger and desire to share Himself, and His life, with us His children.

Know this. He is interested and will listen carefully, no matter how long the story. Here is a secret for you. As your relationship grows with the Lord and you become comfortable sharing with Him, you'll find that He will also share with you His thoughts, His feelings, and His desires. He will guide you and give you His insight on a variety of topics.

To some, this might sound outrageous. But think about it for a moment. Don't we sing songs in church services like "What a Friend We Have in Jesus," and more recently, "I Am a Friend of God?" Are the words of these songs true or not? In the Bible, Jesus is called *"a friend of publicans and sinners."*[2]

So you see Jesus is our Friend. James wrote, *"Abraham believed God, and it was credited to him as righteousness, and he was called God's friend."*[3]

The Revelation

Throughout my lifetime I've heard many preachers describe the Trinity, so I had a general idea; but one day the Lord gave me a revelation describing the Trinity and their relationship with each other, and with us.

Imagine three lit candles, separate with three individual flames. If you point them toward each other and touch the flames together, they become one flame. Three individual flames become one flame, and you can't tell where one flame ends and the other flames begin. They have merged in unity and become one flame.

Our God is three separate personalities, the Father, the Son Lord Jesus, and the Holy Spirit. Yet they are merged in perfect unity as one God. And as the one God, you can't distinguish where one ends and the other begins. They are one God.

The Trinity as Separate Identities

We discussed how they are one, but Father, Lord Jesus, and the Holy Spirit also have three distinctly separate personalities and identities. There is one God the Father, one Lord Jesus Christ, and one Holy Spirit.

The Hebrew word for God is *Elohim,* which is a uni-plural noun meaning Gods. Here is an amazing fact. The word God is used either singular or plural. It is like the word sheep, which also can be used either singular or plural. The Bible says, *"In the beginning God [Gods] created the heaven and the earth."*[4]

Apostle Paul wrote, *"There is one body and one Spirit, just as you were called to one hope when you were called; one Lord, one faith, one baptism; one God and Father of all, who is over all and through all and in all."*[5] In this Scripture the Father, Son, and Spirit are all called God individually.

- The Father is called God: *"Yet for us there is but one God, the Father, from whom all things came and for whom we live...."*[6]

- The Son is called God: *"But about the Son he says, 'Your throne, O God, will last for ever and ever....'"*[7]

- The Holy Spirit is called God: *"Then Peter said, 'Ananias, how is it that Satan has so filled your heart that you have lied to the Holy Spirit.... You have not lied to men but to God."*[8]

Father, Jesus, and the Holy Spirit are separate personalities of deity as to Their position and office.

- Father is the head of Christ: Paul wrote, *"the head of Christ is God."*[9]

- Jesus is the only begotten of the Father: John said, *"Jesus Christ, the Father's Son."*[10]

- The Holy Spirit proceeds from both the Father and the Son: Jesus said, *"And I will pray* [ask] *the Father, and he shall give you another Comforter* [Counselor] *that he may abide with you for ever; even the Spirit of truth."*[11] Moses wrote, *"And the Lord God said, 'The man has now become like one of us, knowing good and evil.'"*[12]

The three of Them—Father, Son (the Word), and Holy Spirit—discussed among Themselves the situation pertaining to Adam's disobedience and subsequent fall and its consequences. Each of the three members of the Godhead has different functions, which they perform in unity together.

Trinity in Unity

Three persons cannot be one person in an ordinary sense, but three can be one in unity. Jesus prayed:

Holy Father, protect them by the power of your name, the name you gave me, so that they may be one as we are one.[13]

That all of them may be one, Father, just as you are in me and I am in you...that they may be one as we are one: I in them and you in me.[14]

They had a plan, a plan to include humanity into this

The Trinity of One

unity of being. Moses wrote, *"Then God said, 'Let us make man in our image, in our likeness.'"*[15] These and many other Scriptures show the total unity of Father, Lord Jesus, and the Holy Spirit. Like the flame that represents the glory of God, you can't tell where one ends and the other begins.

Man as Separate Identity

The Bible says, *"So God created man in his own image, in the image of God he created him; male and female he created them."*[16] The Hebrew word for man is *Adam, Aw-dawm,* and it means a human being, person, individual, or entire species, like mankind.

Like the image of God in which we were created, we are individuals. No two people are exactly alike. Why? Because we were created in their image! The Trinity is similar but not exactly alike. They hold different positions in the Godhead, and we hold different positions in mankind, and in the body of Christ.

God made us as individuals with our own separate identities and wills. God gave man a spirit, which longs for the Spirit of God. Solomon wrote, *"The spirit of man is the candle of the Lord, searching all the inward parts of the belly."*[17]

Man in Unity as the Body of Christ

Man is a naturally social creature who is not happy to be alone. We must have interaction with others. People tend to come together with family, friends, and others of common bond or interest. That's just the way we are because God is that way—and we were created in Their image. Apostle Paul wrote to the church at Corinth, *"For we were all baptized by one Spirit into one body."*[18] This is not a baptism into the Spirit, but into the body of Christ.

> *The body is a unit, though it is made up of many parts; and though all its parts are many, they form one body. So it is with Christ.*[19]

Now you are the body of Christ, and each one of you is a part of it.[20]

So through Christ's death, burial, and resurrection, He has brought us into His body as we accept Him as our Lord and Savior. We are one in unity with each other as the body of Christ, just like our example the Trinity, who are One in unity as God!

Unity in Spiritual Light

The Bible says, *"God is light; in him there is no darkness at all. If we claim to have fellowship with him yet walk in the darkness, we lie and do not live by the truth. But if we walk in the light, as he is in the light, we have fellowship with one another, and the blood of Jesus, his Son, purifies us from all sin."*[21]

In Christ we have unity with God and fellowship with them in the Spirit. In the book of Matthew, the writer describes Christ's glory in the glory of God. Matthew wrote, *"His face shone like the sun, and his clothes became as white as the light."*[22] Here we are shown the Spirit of Christ in perfect unity with the glory of God. Here we are shown a glimpse of the flame, the glory of God in all His holiness. He welcomes us into His glory!

Paul wrote to the church in Corinth, *"And we, who with unveiled faces all the Lord's glory, are being transformed into his likeness with ever-increasing glory, which comes from the Lord, who is the Spirit."*[23] Transformed, in the original Greek, is *metamorphoo,* which means transfigure.[24]

Jesus prayed to the Father, *"I have given them the glory that you gave me, that they may be one as we are one: I in them and you in me."*[25] Through Christ, we are welcomed into the oneness of God. And in perfect unity through Christ, you can't tell where God ends and we begin. Jesus also prayed,

"That all of them may be one, Father, just as you are in me and I am in you."[26]

God Is Light

The Greek word for light is *phos,* which means to shine or make manifest, especially by rays, luminousness, or fire.

One day I was praying in the Spirit and found myself caught up to heaven. Looking around at my surroundings, I saw a great and beautiful lake, which sat in the midst of the most beautiful primeval forest I had ever seen. On the far side of the lake, Father and Lord Jesus were standing facing me. I immediately made my way around the right side of the lake toward them. My heart beat with anticipation and excitement as I picked up the pace, walking as fast as I could without running. I was a little afraid that They might leave, but They didn't. They just stood there with pleasant looks on their faces, patiently waiting for me.

As I approached them, I wanted with every fiber of my being, to fall down on my face before Them as I have many times before in the throne room. But I sensed that it was not what They wanted. No, They were simply happy to see me; as I reached them, They both extended Their arms and embraced me. Of course I also embraced Them, and we ended up in a group hug, which included the Holy Spirit.

After a time of greeting and fellowship, we turned and began to walk away from the lake and toward the forest. Mere words cannot describe the feeling of walking with Father on my right, Lord Jesus on my left, and the Holy Spirit behind and above us. We walked up a slight incline on a natural path, about thirty yards wide. The path was covered in beautiful grass that looked like it had never been stepped upon. On either side of the path was a forest of trees, which had to be at least one hundred feet tall.

All that I saw looked untouched and primitive, as I imagine our earth appeared in the days of Eden. Even though we were walking uphill, I could do it effortlessly, with no heavy breathing. Hallelujah! We spoke not a word, but an understanding passed between us. We shared a knowing of love and acceptance in the Spirit.

Father reached over and took my right hand in His left, and then Lord Jesus took my left hand in His right. I felt like a little child, safe in the hands of his Father and elder Brother.

In the forest to my right, a large bird perched about halfway up the trees. With about two flaps of its wings, it glided across the path in front of us with ease and disappeared into the forest on our left. This bird had a long, slender body, a long neck, and a wingspan of about twelve feet. This bird, our surroundings, and we basked in perfect peace.

We basked in perfect peace.

After walking for a while, I noticed fire in the forest. At first there was a flicker of flame on the ground in the forest on our right, then in the trees on our left. If I had seen this on earth, I would have been alarmed, but here I felt safe in Their hands, literally. The farther up the path we walked the larger the flames rose, until the bottom half of the forest was engulfed on both sides.

I looked to Father, and then over to Lord Jesus, but They, with their heads held high, looked straight ahead without saying a word. A quiet confidence exuded from Them, giving me peace while the forest burned around us. Looking at the fire, I wondered about the bird and other wildlife that may reside in the forest. No sooner than the thought crossed my mind, Father spoke, "They are fine. They are part of it."

I was glad to hear that they were safe, but I couldn't understand how they were part of the burning forest. I searched the trees with my eyes for any signs of wildlife but saw nothing. An amazing phenomenon was happening. The fire was not consuming the trees! Though burning with giant flames, the forest remained intact. Also there was no smoke. It reminded me of the burning bush that Moses encountered.[27]

I was awestruck by this. Here I was walking with the Lord Jesus, Father, and the Holy Spirit not by a burning bush, but in a burning forest! As I closed my eyes and bowed my head in wonder, I felt a warm sensation on my hands. I opened my eyes and was startled to see that my hands were on fire!

My right hand that Father held was on fire up to my wrist, as was His. No pain was felt whatsoever, just a gentle, comforting, warm sensation. Looking up to Father, He returned my gaze and smiled, His pleasant countenance filled with anticipation as if to say, if you think this is something, just wait! My eyes must have widened as big as saucers as I realized that my hand and Father's hand had become one in the fire!

Next there was a tug on my left hand. I looked down and my left hand, which was being held by Jesus, was also in flames. I felt the same warm sensation and oneness with the hand of Christ. I looked up at Jesus and He too was grinning from ear to ear. It was easy to tell that He was enjoying my reaction.

I looked from my right hand to my left, back and forth while Father and Lord Jesus looked straight ahead with heads held high. Eventually I settled in and accepted this holy state of being with God. As we continued to walk, I lifted my head, closed my eyes, took a deep breath, and tried to relax.

After a few more steps, I opened my eyes and noticed that the flames were about three quarters of the way up the trees on either side. At the same time, I felt the warm sensation on my hands move up to my forearms. Looking down, I discovered the flames had risen from my hand up to my elbow, and Father's arm was aflame as well. My left arm was the same, as was the arm of Lord Jesus.

Father, Lord Jesus, the Holy Spirit, and I were one burning flame.

The farther up the path we walked, the higher the flames climbed up the trees, and up the three of us until eventually the trees and the path were completely engulfed in flames. As I turned my gaze back to us, I found that we also were completely engulfed in flames from head to toe. Father, Lord Jesus, the Holy Spirit, and I were one burning flame.

The oneness that I felt with Them is difficult to explain. Although I could feel and sense the individuality of my person, I could also feel the person of Father, from the inside, in total unity as if I had merged with Him. I couldn't distinguish where I ended and Father began, or where He ended and I began.

While I was trying to process this in my mind, I looked to my left and saw myself in flames with Lord Jesus. Over my shoulder I saw the Holy Spirit as well. We were all four merged in unity in the fire of the glory of God. I felt myself in and through Them, and Them in and through me. We were one and four!

Who am I that God, my God, would choose to love me? I gave up asking Them that question years ago. But one thing I know, this relationship, this oneness in unity, is not only what They want; but it's what They're all about. Listen carefully. To fellowship with Their children is their dream. When you submit your will to God and seek Their face, you are making Their dream come true!

I'll tell you it's humbling, but guess what? This is how He feels about you! God wants you! Father, Lord Jesus, and the Holy Spirit want to include you in this unity with Them.

When I think about Their love for us, and the sacrifices

that They've made for you and I, dear reader, I am awestruck. We don't deserve it, and we can't earn it. Their love for us just is, and They want each of us to know.

What I have described here is just the tip of the iceberg. I previously illustrated how the flames of the three candles become one flame when put together, and compared it to the unity of the Father, Son, and Holy Spirit. The Lord wants us to see and experience the fact that when we are born again, our spirits become alive, born into God.

In other words, our little candle flame is placed into Their flame and we become one with Them in the Spirit! Already, untold millions have become one with Them in the Spirit. Dear reader, if you are born again, then your flame is merged in Their flame as well. You are born again into Their Spirit where you belong. Ask the Holy Spirit to open your spiritual eyes to see in the Spirit. He will!

Chapter 4

The Three Faces of God

My maternal grandfather, William Arrowood, was my earliest and most significant male role model when I was a boy. In my mind I can still hear his laugh as if it were only yesterday. He's been with the Lord for more than twenty years, but his godly life is an example I'll always remember and try to emulate. He was a great man of God. When I was a boy, we would take long walks together to the store or the barbershop, and he often spoke of the Lord.

One thing I will never forget is his instruction to seek the face of the Lord. He must have told me that dozens of times; and as a kid, I thought that he was just encouraging me to pray. But as an adult, I knew that there was something more, a deeper experience with God. Granddaddy was known in our family for having dreams from God, and he always started his day before dawn, in prayer and Bible study.

It wasn't until years after he passed away that I finally understood what seeking the face of God could mean. We already know that to seek the face of God in prayer causes us to come into His presence, which is of utmost importance. Many believers go through their prayer life feeling His presence when we seek His face, and that is marvelous.

But I encourage you, dear reader, to press on to a revelation that's waiting for you according to God's will. That is to have the eyes of your understanding opened to actually see His face in the Spirit as you seek Him. Yes, I understood this when praying in the Spirit, and I saw the face of the Lord. Some may ask, "What does He look like?" I'll try to answer that in more detail later, but for now, suffice it to say it's like describing a Pacific Ocean sunset. Beautiful, amazing, breathtaking, and just the way it's supposed to be.

The Bible gives us instruction and encouragement to seek the face of the Lord: *"Look to the Lord and his strength; seek his face always."*[1] *"If my people, who are called by my name, will humble themselves and pray and seek my face...."*[2] The Word also encourages all of us, *"Let your face shine on your servant."*[3]

As you can see, we are told in God's Word to seek His face! Now I don't want to discourage anyone from seeking His presence by faith without a vision, but I want to encourage you to seek the Lord in the fullest sense. Don't let the enemy discourage you. You are special to the Lord and He desires to fellowship in the Spirit with you. He has *"placed before you an open door that no one can shut,"*[4] so walk through, look around, and don't look back.

People who have seen the Lord usually don't feel worthy to have had the experience. They might ask, "Who am I? Why me?" The answer is quite simple. The Lord looks into the heart of the person who seeks Him.

He doesn't deem us worthy by who we are in this world or what position we might hold. He deems us worthy by virtue of the fact that we are His sons and daughters, and He loves us with an insatiable love, desiring above all else to fellowship with us. In this life it's done in the Spirit. That's it. His love makes us worthy, period. After all, His love sent Lord Jesus to the cross for us, and Christ's love held Him there.

So I sat in my study, kicked back in my chair and

contemplated this chapter. Should I, or should I not discuss seeing the face of God? Well, the Lord's answer was that I definitely should. Then my question was how should I tell and explain it? You see, I really want the Lord to be glorified, and you, dear Reader, to be blessed. I did not want to mess this up, so I sat there, waiting on the Lord, contemplating this with fear and trembling.

Then a sound came from my computer, which was softly playing an Internet radio station from Hawaii. The sound was a low male baritone voice singing an old love song, "The first time ever I saw your face." I just had to laugh. The Lord definitely has a sense of humor, confirming the answer to my dilemma that way. I'm telling you, walking with the Lord in the Spirit is an adventure. So I said with a chuckle, "OK, Lord, I'll tell about the first time ever I saw Your face."

November 19, 1992

My brother in the Lord and I were praying in the Spirit when we were caught up to heaven. I saw steps leading up to the temple of God. The Holy Spirit brought me up the steps and into the Holy Place. Inside it was dark. A mist that filled the room caused the darkness. Standing perfectly still, I quietly observed the mist slowly swirling around me.

I focused my gaze to see through the mist as it receded slightly, revealing the face of Jesus directly in front of my face, almost nose to nose! The dark mist swirled around and between us, sometimes blocking my view as He stepped to my right and stood close by me. I turned my head to the right and looked directly at Him. He was looking straight ahead, which allowed me to see the side of His face. Then He turned and looked directly at me, face to face, just inches apart.

I was completely stunned and amazed by the sight of Him. I couldn't stop looking. He was so beautiful! I stood quietly beside Him for a time, holding His hand. After a while,

Jesus turned and faced forward, as did I.

As the Lord Jesus and I looked into the mist, it thinned somewhat. A few feet from us stood the figure of a man. An opening in the mist revealed Him from the waist up, standing facing toward our right.

He was completely white. He wore a robe of white. His hair and beard were white, as was His skin. Every part of Him was the same color of white! I'm not saying His skin was Caucasian. This white was unlike any color I had ever seen before. It was the bright light of glory. We beheld the Father! This was God almighty!

Gazing closely I could see the texture of His skin, His hair, and His beard. Here I stood…in heaven…with Lord Jesus…looking at Father! Looking at Father's face close up, I could see the remarkable resemblance to Lord Jesus. Side by side, I could see them as Father and Son. They both have some wrinkles, or crows' feet, around their eyes. Father's were slightly more pronounced.

I studied the texture and even the pores of His skin. Father's vibrant face was filled with love and compassion. Although this was the first time I saw His face, He looked somewhat familiar. He looked just like He was supposed to look.

Now I understand what it means in the Bible when it refers to God walking in darkness. The glory of God is pure light; and in His presence, darkness surrounds His glory. Moses experienced this in the desert wilderness:

> *The people remained at a distance, while Moses approached the thick darkness where God was. Then the Lord said to Moses, "Tell the Israelites this: 'You have seen for yourselves that I have spoken to you from heaven.'"*[5]

King Solomon said, *"The Lord has said that he would*

dwell in a dark cloud."[6]

This discovery was a great surprise to me. I had no idea that darkness surrounded His glory until seeing it for myself in the Spirit, and then confirming it in the Bible. Since then, I have seen Father on many occasions. Again I say to you, dear reader, my prayer and desire is for you to experience the same. Believe me, this is the will of God!

December 17, 1992

On this day I had an experience with the Holy Spirit and saw Him as He really is. I saw the face of the precious Holy Spirit. Yes, He does have a face! But of course He does, He's the third Person of the Godhead.

I was praying in the Spirit when I found myself in the heavenly realm, standing in the Holy Place in the temple of God. The mist was swirling and the glory of God was everywhere. Out of the swirling mist and glory of God, a face emerged. Never will I forget the first time I saw that beautiful face.

I saw His left profile first. Then He turned to His left and faced me. We looked each other straight in the eyes. His face was strong yet childlike, expressionless and yet full of love and compassion. His countenance was mighty, but also humble. There wasn't a hair on His face or head, not even eyebrows, but He looked very handsome and distinguished. His face came out of the mist of the glory cloud. It was as if His body was the glory cloud, yet He had no physical body that I could see. However, seeing His face as it came out of the glory cloud felt very natural, all-powerful, and yet sweet like a child. The Holy Spirit has a face!

As I stared intently at Him, His face went into me. I can't explain how, but I could see His face within me. He drew me into the glory cloud and I saw the Holy Spirit as a swirling mass, a column of fire. He drew me up into the fire, into God and His realm, which is called the third heaven. I felt like I could see eternity from one end to the other. Mere words cannot explain what I saw, but I will say this, God is a consuming fire, mighty and powerful. The Bible says that God is light, and in Him is no darkness at all.[7]

God made heaven a place where He can meet with man, a place where He can come down from His glory realm of light, and walk among His children and have fellowship with us. After I came back down to heaven, I stood and faced the Trinity. God the Father stood beside the Lord Jesus His Son, with the glory cloud surrounding Them and the face of the Holy Spirit between them. I'll never forget the first time I saw Them together. They are my family, our family, and I love Them very much.

Everyday Prayer

When you have a vision while praying in the Spirit, like the one just described, there is certain clarity of sight. Your spiritual eyes can see as clearly in the Spirit realm as your physical eyes in the natural realm. But there are also times when you don't see clearly. Like the apostle Paul described, we see through a glass darkly. Let me give you an example. You are praying with your eyes closed, so naturally you see nothing but darkness. Well, out of that darkness an image may appear.

When you seek the face of the Lord, He, or They, will appear out of that darkness. This can happen in many ways. Sometimes a faint outline of a forehead and nose might appear. At other times, a faint image of a right or left profile will appear. Images appear for a moment or two, sometimes less. It can also be like a flash, where you see the face clearly for a split second and then it's gone, but the image remains in your mind. Whatever manner They choose to manifest Themselves, They usually appear long enough for you to know that They are there. This is a comforting blessing.

On occasion, in prayer with my eyes closed, a dot of light as small as a pinhole will appear in the darkness. Then it gets bigger and bigger until the face of the Lord comes out of the light. The face of the Lord Jesus is then surrounded by glorious light and is close enough to be seen clearly. In a few moments, He moves back into the darkness until there's just a pinhole of light left, and then He's gone.

Sometimes the face of the Holy Spirit appears by Himself, but usually They appear One by One, and then together, long enough for me to see Them before they leave. For me, this has become an everyday prayer. I am not satisfied unless I see one or all three faces.

One morning, after I had been in the Spirit all night, I awoke before dawn, and in the darkness, the face of the Holy Spirit appeared directly in front of my face. In that split second between consciousness and slumber, His face was so clear and real that I was startled and jumped! To fellowship in the Spirit with Them is the ultimate.

The Lord always confirms these things through His Word, as I have already shared Scriptures that encourage us to seek His face. The Hebrew word used in the Scriptures for face is *paneh,* which means, "face, as the part that turns." And I have already noted that when I see Them, They are usually turning and giving me a panorama of Their face from every profile. The Hebrew word *paneh* comes from the word *paniym,* which is a plural word that is always used singular.

Wow! What a confirmation. I had no idea that the Hebrew dictionary would describe the word face that way, and that the word for face is plural yet used singular. It's just like God the Trinity, plural yet singular. God's Word is awesome!

I must confess that there have been times over the years when I have allowed our fellowship in the Spirit to lapse. Busy, earthly days take their toll, but eventually it will hit me that I haven't been in Their presence lately, and my heart will break. A strong longing and desire comes over me. I actually get homesick for Them, so I seek Them and guess what? They are always there to welcome me. Hallelujah! I may fail Them, but They never fail me!

In his book on intercession, Rees Howell talks about being disobedient and losing the face of God. As you seek Their face, your experience may be similar to mine, but don't box Them in. Just ask Them to have Their way with you. God has a unique relationship and an experience designed expressly for you. They offer an intimate relationship that is unique to you and Them.

No One Has Seen God?

Now here is an interesting statement. The Bible says, *"No one has ever seen God."*[8] This is a plain and simple statement that contradicts everything I have just said, right? Many Christians will read that verse and give up any hope of seeing the Lord. Some pastors will even preach that visions of the Lord are not for today, and that those who claim to have seen Him are, shall we say, not quite right.

So, let's take a look at what the same writer, John, wrote in the same book:

> *That which was from the beginning, which we have heard, which we have seen with our eyes, which we have looked at and our hands have touched—this we proclaim concerning the Word of life. The life appeared; we have seen it and testify to it, and we proclaim to you the eternal life, which was with the Father and has appeared to us. We proclaim to you what we have seen and heard, so that you also may have fellowship with us. And our fellowship is with the Father and with his Son, Jesus Christ. We write this to make our joy complete.*[9]

So, does the Word of God contradict itself? Let us face this question head-on. First of all, there are many examples throughout the Bible of God being seen.

> *So Jacob called the place Peniel, saying, "It is because I saw God face to face, and yet my life was spared."[10]*
>
> *Moses and Aaron, Nadab and Abihu, and the seventy elders of Israel went up and saw the God of Israel. Under his feet was something like a pavement made of sapphire, clear as the sky itself. But God did not raise his hand against these leaders of the Israelites; they saw God, and they ate and drank.[11]*
>
> *The Lord would speak to Moses face to face, as a man speaks with his friend.[12]*

As Stephen was being stoned, he exclaimed, *"Look,"* he said, *"I see heaven open and the Son of Man standing at the right hand of God."*[13]

As these Scriptures and many others attest to people seeing God, and the apostle John himself wrote in the same book that he has seen the Lord Jesus and fellowshipped in the light with the Father and Lord Jesus, then when John wrote that no one has seen God, he must have been referring to something else. He may be referring to seeing all the glory of God as Yahweh, the Three in One, with the natural eyes.

Moses said to God, *"Now show me your glory."*[14] Moses had already seen God face to face, but he wanted to see Him in all His glory. God told Moses that He would cause all His goodness to pass in front of him and would proclaim His name in Moses' presence, but he could not see God's face in that state and live. So God put Moses in a protected cleft in a rock and covered Moses with His own hand as He passed. Then, God removed His hand and allowed Moses to see His back as He passed. God told Moses that he couldn't see His face in His glory and live.

Other Scriptures plainly attest to the fact that God will appear in an expression of Himself, a form, which humans can see. Sometimes with the natural eyes like He did with Moses and the seventy elders, and sometimes with the spiritual eyes as He did in the light as John described. By the way, that Greek word for light, *phos,* also means fire.

Why would the Bible encourage us to seek His face and give us so many examples of those who did, if it were impossible? It simply wouldn't. Some say that seeing Him was only for those special few prophets and apostles of old, not for us, and not for today. That is simply not true, for the heart of God is to fellowship with all of His children, and He has made it possible through the precious Holy Spirit.

Call unto Me

The Church, the body of Christ, is crying out for a closer relationship. Believers want to fellowship in the Spirit with the Lord. You can hear the yearning in popular modern-day songs such as: "I See the Lord," "Open the Eyes of My Heart," and "I Can Only Imagine." There's a desire in the body of Christ for intimacy and fellowship in the Spirit with Them—the Three and One.

The Lord encouraged Jeremiah by saying, *"Call to me and I will answer you and tell you great and unsearchable things you do not know."*[15]

Apostle Paul wrote:

I keep asking that the God of our Lord Jesus Christ, the glorious Father, may give you the Spirit of wisdom and revelation, so that you may know him better. I pray also that the eyes of your heart may be enlightened in order that you may know the hope to which he has called you, the riches of his glorious inheritance in the saints.[16]

Paul is praying, "Open the eyes of their heart, Lord." This is also my prayer for you: "Dear Father, I ask You right now to open the spiritual eyes of this dear reader. Show Yourself so that this reader might fellowship in the Spirit with You. In Jesus' name I pray, amen."

Now, like any gift of the Lord, having your spiritual eyes opened is like receiving salvation, sanctification, the baptism of the Holy Spirit, and ministry gifts. Jesus said, *"Therefore I tell you, whatever you ask for in prayer, believe that you have received it, and it will be yours."*[17]

So ask, believe, and receive the gift of having your spiritual eyes opened.

Chapter 5

The Mystery of the Gospel

The apostle Paul wrote, *"The mystery that has been kept hidden for ages and generations, but is now disclosed to the saints. To them God has chosen to make known among the Gentiles the glorious riches of this mystery, which is* **Christ in you, the hope of glory***."*[1]

The Bible says, *"Unto you it is given to know the mystery of the kingdom of God."*[2] Paul's revelation of the mystery of the gospel, Christ in us and us in Christ, is a cord that is woven throughout the New Testament.

Sometimes this cord of revelation is very plainly stated, but other times it is subtle, as if it's simply understood by the recipients of his writings. The Holy Spirit is calling the Church to grasp this revelation and receive it afresh and anew.

Once the revelation of who we are in Christ is received, it is plain to see it throughout the Scriptures. Let us pray the prayer of the apostle Paul:

> *That the God of our Lord Jesus Christ, the glorious Father, may give you the Spirit of wisdom and revelation, so that you may know him better. I pray also that the eyes of your heart may be enlightened in order that you may know the hope to which he has called you, the riches of his glorious inheritance in the saints, and his incomparably great power for us who believe.*[3]

"Christ in you, the hope of glory," these words in Colossians are the secret and the answer to the mystery of the gospel. It is the climax, the culmination, and the achieved goal of mankind since Granddaddy Adam lost his spiritual connection and fellowship with God, the Trinity, in the Garden of Eden.

Adam

Apostle Paul wrote, *"Therefore, just as sin entered the world through one man, and death through sin, and in this way death came to all men, because all sinned."*[4]

All humanity suffered the consequences of Adam's disobedience. Before I was born, I was physically in my father. Before my father was born, he was in his father, my grandfather. So then, I was in my father, and in him, in my grandfather, and so on all the way back through the generations to Granddaddy Adam. The whole human race was in him when he sinned. Adam did not act as a single person, but as the whole human race.

When he fell we all fell with Him because we were all in him. God's covenant with Adam was a covenant with us all—blessings if Adam obeyed, and curses if he disobeyed. *"For since death came through a man, the resurrection of the dead comes also through a man. For as in Adam all die, so in Christ all will be made alive."*[5] By Adam's disobedience we suffer death, but by Christ's obedience we gain life, the very life of God in us! But why did this all happen? Why did Granddaddy Adam have to sin and fall? Let's go back a bit.

In the beginning, everything that was created by God was done for man, with man in mind. Father wanted to make a world that would cradle man, a world where he had everything, a world of beauty, splendor, and glory. And God walked with him in union. No other creation was made in the image of God but man. He was given dominion and authority over the earth.

Gardening with Father

Sometimes while praying in the Spirit, I have been privileged to commune with Father in His garden paradise in heaven. It is located behind His house and is most incredible and enjoyable. Father loves to work in His garden. He will groom plants, take a cutting and plant it in some other area of His garden, or maybe graft it into another plant. He is always tinkering, experimenting, and creating in His garden. As a matter of fact, if you want to find Father in heaven, look in the throne room first to see if He is there conducting business. If not, then look to see if He is fellowshipping with His people, His children, around the heavenly city. If not there, you will probably find Him tinkering in His garden. It might sound funny but it is the truth.

I love spending time with Him in His garden paradise, which is located behind His house. He has taught me many things in His garden. For instance, while in His garden, He taught me about the origin of the Garden of Eden.

Did you know that God did not speak the Garden of Eden into existence as He did the rest of the world? Look carefully at the Scripture: *"Now the Lord God had planted a garden in the east, in Eden."*[6]

You see, He planted the Garden of Eden Himself with His very own hands. He did on earth what He loves to do in heaven. He showed me how He took plants from His own garden and planted them in Eden. Some were whole plants and some were cuttings from His plants. As I sat back and watched Him work in His garden, it made so much sense. I love gardening on earth, but to garden with Him in His garden paradise is ultimate fulfillment. I love it when He lets me help. I especially love when the project is done and we just sit and look at His handiwork, enjoying small talk between us. I can imagine how it must have been for them, Father and Adam, as

Father taught Adam how to work the Garden, and then later walk together in the cool of the evening and share small talk.

Satan's Plan

What happened to destroy that relationship was so tragic, and so unnecessary. We know from the Scriptures how Lucifer, Satan, the bright and shining angel, fell from heaven and took a third of the angels with him. Well, he knew that he could never actually overthrow God. In fact he never tried to overthrow God; he lifted himself in pride and aspired to be like God, not to be God. He wanted to be worshipped, to be *like* the Most High, not to *be* the Most High.

Isaiah wrote about Lucifer, *"I will ascend the heights of the clouds: I will be like the most High."*[7] When he saw that God created a man in His image and had given that man, that human race, dominion and authority over the earth, he hatched a diabolical plan. He thought that if he could get Adam to disobey God and eat of the tree of the knowledge of good and evil, then God would somehow forgive Adam and make an exception to His Word. If God did this for Adam, then He, in His justice, would also have to make an exception for him, the devil.

In this way Satan would wrest the dominion and authority from Adam, from man, and have it for himself, making man subservient to him. What an outrage! He convinced Adam, through Eve, to disobey God and pursue self-glory and pride. Just as God promised, Adam, Eve, and all humanity in them died. We know the story.

God was as good as His Word, and subsequently man lost his dominion and authority. It hurt Father so much to see what man became after this. It hurt so badly. Man's spirit died. He was filled with death and spiritual darkness. It was a sad moment when they hid themselves from God, with whom they had walked in such perfect unity. God felt the loss, as well as

Adam, now that Adam was actually afraid of God.

Man Is Fallen

Apostle Paul wrote to the church in Rome:

There is no one righteous, not even one; there is no one who understands, no one who seeks God. All have turned away, they have together become worthless; there is no one who does good, not even one. Their throats are open graves; their tongues practice deceit.[8]

After the fall, man's condition became despicable, pitiful, and beastly. Although man knew better, he became like the devil in a lowly, lost, hopeless state, the very opposite of God his Father, and more like Satan, his adopted father. He lost the attributes of God and personified the attributes of Satan. He broke the covenant and earned death.

It broke the heart of God to see what his man had become. Man, a creature made to walk in the glory realm in fellowship with Father, Lord Jesus, and the Holy Spirit had become a horror.

Paul wrote, *"The god of this age has blinded the minds of unbelievers."*[9]

Because of whom man became, his inheritance in God was lost. The ruthless evil ruler of this world blinded man. We were so very lost and without hope. Man had lost the image of God and was remade in the image of his adopted father, the devil.

The Bible says, *"Remember that at that time you were separate from Christ, excluded from citizenship in Israel and foreigners to the covenants of the promise, without hope and without God in the world."*[10] Man was estranged with no hope, no rights, and no fellowship with God.

What Satan didn't understand was that God loved man. His very life had gone into man. Humanity was His family, made to walk in fellowship, holiness, and the purity of God. But the mind of man was on evil constantly and actually hated God for no reason at all.

The strength of dominion that man possessed was now perverted and used by man to kill and control other men. Men were killing men and entering into every manner of perversion. It broke the very heart of God.

I was in the Spirit one day with Father, spending time with Him showing me around His house in heaven. "Let Me show you something else," Father said. He took me over to a tall table, about chest high, on the opposite side of the room. On the table was a sculpture of a man, a bust from the shoulders up. The face looked vaguely familiar. As a matter of fact, he favored Lord Jesus, except that he had no beard or facial hair.

"Is this Lord Jesus?" I asked.

"No, Son," He replied. "That's My son Adam, your grandfather, many generations removed."

"Wow!" I said. "He is beautiful. Who made this, Father?"

"I did," He replied. "However, if you look closely, you'll see a flaw."

I examined it carefully and on the base of the skull in the back, I found a crack.

"What caused this crack, Father?" I asked.

"You found it!" He replied.

With that, He picked up the bust, walked over to a big chair and sat down, holding the bust carefully. I sat cross-legged on the floor, at His feet, and asked Him to tell me about the flaw. He proceeded to tell me how He cracked the bust after He made it and placed it on the table here in the house. When Adam fell and he and Eve were put out of the Garden,

Father came here, looked at this bust and wept. In anger and frustration He slapped the bust off the table and when it hit the floor it cracked. Father picked it up and lovingly placed it back on the table, but from then on, the bust and Adam had a flaw.

"Oh, how many times I have held this until My Son Jesus brought him back here again. Other than My Son Jesus, I have loved Adam the longest," Father said.

So you see God didn't stop loving Adam when he fell. When He was separated from Adam, Father had his likeness in the form of a sculptured bust to gaze upon. His love never changes. The time came when Father, Lord Jesus, and the Holy Spirit couldn't take it any longer. They felt like man had suffered enough.

Christ on Earth

"But when the time had fully come, God sent his Son, born of a woman, born under law."[11] God ended the crisis of man's horrible existence by sending His Son Lord Jesus in the flesh into our circumstances to do what Adam did not do and what we could not do for ourselves.

> *Since the children have flesh and blood, he too shared in their humanity so that by his death he might break the power of him who holds the power of death—that is, the devil.*[12]

Jesus had to become flesh and blood in order to represent flesh and blood in His sacrifice. He had to suffer as a man to redeem men. Having "walked in our shoes" in every way, He understands man, not just from a divine knowledge, but because of life He experienced as a man.

All redemptive covenants were ratified by the death of a victim. God redeemed man by a human sacrifice of infinite value, by preparing a body, the body of His own Son. He replaced the old animal sacrifices of the first covenant with the perfect human sacrifice of His Son, thus establishing the new and everlasting covenant.

Christ, Our Substitute

To the church in Rome Paul wrote, *"But God demonstrates his own love for us in this: While we were still sinners, Christ died for us."*[13] God loves us so much—even in our lost rebellious condition—that He gave Jesus in our place to bear and pay the penalty for our sins. We were unable to pay the price for our sin, so how can we ever repay so wonderful a sacrifice? We can't, but we can give Him our life, which He bought with His life, and allow Him to live in and through us.

Paul wrote, *"For just as through the disobedience of the one man the many were made sinners, so also through the obedience of the one man the many will be made righteous."*[14] Since we were born exact copies of our flawed Granddaddy Adam, we must accept the sacrifice of Christ as He took our place on the cross and did what we were unable to do for our doomed selves.

"God made him who had no sin [Lord Jesus] *to be sin for us, so that in him we might become the righteousness of God."*[15] As our substitute, He became sin, and we became righteous. This was done by a sovereign act of the Father.

The Lord Jesus, the Son of Man, loved being a man. He referred to Himself many times as "the Son of Man." It had to be a man who walked in victory. It had to be mankind in Him, for the Lord Jesus stood for us all, even as the first Adam did. The fate of the human race rested on Him. Alone at night, the weight of it was almost more than He could bear.

In the Spirit, He shared with me that there were many times when He prayed all night to His Father because the burden was so heavy, and Father came through for Him. Even after He was tempted in the desert by the devil, Father sent angels to strengthen Him.

He told me that when men said mean and insulting things about Him it hurt Him just like it hurts us. When His disciples fled, even though He knew that they must, it still hurt Him. It hurt when nobody stood with Him and He was alone.

A Vision at the Cross

What happened on Mount Calvary on that fateful day was unspeakably important to mankind. We know the story, but do we take it personally? It became very personal to me one day while praying in the Spirit. I was taken there.

I found myself standing on Mount Calvary. It was dark. Furious black clouds were swirling around my head so low to the earth I could almost reach up and touch them. Thunder resounded as flashes of lightning illuminated the scene ever so quickly. With one flash of lightning I could see Roman soldiers gathered in a circle, each on one knee. They were gambling and laughing.

Another flash of lightning came and I saw a small group of people, mostly women, weeping and waving their arms as if swatting flies. But they weren't swatting flies. They were striking out in the air against those soldiers, begging them to stop what they were doing.

With another flash of lightning, I almost jumped back as I saw Him. The Lord Jesus stepped up to me. I knew He was in the process of being crucified, but somehow He stopped everything and walked over to me. I did not touch Him, but we were almost nose to nose as He stood there breathing very deeply, out of breath, as if He had been running. He was certainly close enough to see in the dark, but another flash of lightning lit His features and the sight of His condition filled me with horror.

He wore no robe and it seemed as if every inch of His chest and shoulders were cut with deep gashes. He was bleeding and sweating. And the smell, the smell was wretched. In spite of the condition of His body, His eyes remained strong and in control. As I stood there and beheld Him, I felt badly. I looked at myself in clean clothes, clean hair, clean-shaven with the smell of fresh cologne, and there He was in that horrible condition.

I felt badly because I was doing nothing, and here my Lord was doing everything. I had interrupted His work on the cross. And it was work, my work, and my cross. I should be doing something! That was all I could think about. It wasn't fair that He was doing it all, doing it all for me, and I didn't lift a finger to help. My sense of obligation to Him was enormous, almost crushing. As I stood there and tried to relate this to Him, He put His right hand on my left shoulder, leaned over toward me cheek to cheek and said to me, "It's all right. I've got this." He made me understand that it was His work and He would finish it.

He leaned back, His hand still on my shoulder, and smiled. With blood and sweat pouring down the sides of His face, He smiled! He was about to die for me, and there was nothing I could do about it. At that moment it became very personal. He wasn't just dying for humanity. He wasn't only dying for the world. No, He was dying for me!

Chapter 6

Jesus in My Mirror

Don't you know that all of us who were baptized into Christ Jesus were baptized into his death? We were therefore buried with him through baptism into death in order that, just as Christ was raised from the dead through the glory of the Father, we too may live a new life. If we have been united with him like this in his death, we will certainly also be united with him in his resurrection. For we know that our old self was crucified with him so that the body of sin might be done away with, that we should no longer be slaves to sin—because anyone who has died has been freed from sin. Now if we died with Christ, we believe that we will also live with him.[1]

Identical in Christ

We were baptized into Jesus Christ. We were crucified with Him, died with Him, raised with Him, and now we live with Him. Everything of His is ours.

The Bible says, *"The Spirit himself testifies with our spirit that we are God's children. Now if we are children, then we are heirs—heirs of God and co-heirs with Christ, if indeed we share in his sufferings in order that we may also share in his glory."*[2] Having become one with Him, we are one in the spirit and children of God. Otherwise, how could we have the Spirit of God? *"For since death came through a man, the resurrection of the dead comes also through a man. For* as in Adam all die, so in Christ all will be made alive."[3] Our identification with Adam assured our death, so it is fair that our new identity in Christ assures us life.

Paul wrote, *"I have been crucified with Christ and I no longer live, but Christ lives in me. The life I live in the body, I live by faith in the Son of God, who loved me and gave himself for me."*[4] We died in Him, and He lives in us.

> *For in Christ all the fullness of the Deity lives in bodily form, and you have been given fullness in Christ, who is the head over every power and authority. In him you were also circumcised, in the putting off of the sinful nature, not with a circumcision done by the hands of men but with the circumcision done by Christ, having been buried with him in baptism and raised with him through your faith in the power of God, who raised him from the dead. When you were dead in your sins and in the uncircumcision of your sinful nature, God made you alive with Christ. He forgave us all our sins.*[5]

In Him, we are also identified with Father and the Holy Spirit. Paul wrote the church in Colosse, *"Since, then, you have been raised with Christ, set your hearts on things above, where Christ is, seated at the right hand of God. Set your minds on things above, not on earthly things. For you died, and your life is now hidden with Christ in God."*[6]

One day while praying in the Spirit, I found myself in heaven lying on the altar of God, covered in the blood of Jesus with the fire of the Holy Spirit above me in a column. As the column of fire descended upon me, I felt the cleansing, purifying glory of God. When it was over and the fire lifted, I felt pure and holy, a living sacrifice.

I noticed at the foot of the altar stood a large mirror. It was a full-length antique "looking glass" on a large frame that allowed itself to be tilted forward or backward. I rose to my feet and stepped over to it to see how I looked. To my surprise, when I looked in the mirror I didn't see myself. I saw the Lord Jesus! I tilted the frame down to see if, in fact, I was looking through a window, but no, it was a mirror. When I moved, He moved. I was looking at myself—but I was seeing Christ. He and I were one; He in me and I in Him.

"Now we see but a poor reflection as in a mirror; then we shall see face to face."[7] Apostle Paul also wrote, *"And we, who with unveiled faces all reflect the Lord's glory, are being transformed into his likeness with ever-increasing glory, which comes from the Lord, who is the Spirit."*[8] And, *"When Christ, who is your life, appears, then you also will appear with him in glory."*[9] Being identified with Him, we must realize where we are. We are in Him, part of Him, in heaven, on the right hand of God right now!

New Life in Christ

Paul wrote to the Romans, *"But if Christ is in you, then even though your body is subject to death because of sin, the Spirit gives life because of righteousness. And if the Spirit of him who raised Jesus from the dead is living in you, he who raised Christ from the dead will also give life to your mortal bodies because of his Spirit who lives in you."*[10]

Because of God in us, our flesh is dead and our spirit is alive. That life will quicken our dead bodies into resurrection. *"But he who unites himself with the Lord is one with him in spirit."*[11] We are alive spiritually because of our union with Christ. We are now one in life, His life. Again, Paul wrote to the church in Corinth, *"For since death came through a man, the resurrection of the dead comes also through a man. For as in Adam all die, so in Christ all will be made alive."*[12] By Adam's disobedience we suffer death, but by Christ's obedience we gain life. Paul continued, *"So we fix our eyes not on what is seen, but on what is unseen. For what is seen is temporary, but what is unseen is eternal."*[13]

Our new life is eternal, not seen with natural eyes, but through spiritual eyes. *"Therefore, if anyone is in Christ, he is a new creation; the old has gone, the new has come!"*[14] We truly have new life in Christ. All of our old life has passed away. We have become new people in every way, from our past to our future.

To the church at Ephesus Paul wrote, *"For we are God's workmanship, created in Christ Jesus to do good works, which God prepared in advance for us to do."*[15] We are new life because God made us new by His Word. We are in Christ so that we may continue in His works. *"Put on the new self, created to be like God in true righteousness and holiness."*[16]

This new life is Christ's life. We are to become Christlike—Christians renewed in His righteousness and true holiness. What is being Christlike? What are His attributes? With His life in us, we have the ability, privilege, and responsibility for those attributes to manifest in and through our lives.

The Bible says, *"And have put on the new self, which is being renewed in knowledge in the image of its Creator."*[17] Since our old life in Adam has been put off and our new life in Christ has been put on, then act like it. Dear reader, put off the fleshly chains that have held you, and put on the spiritual graces that are the holy and lovely attributes of our new life in Christ.

Paul wrote, *"May God himself, the God of peace, sanctify you through and through. May your whole spirit, soul and body be kept blameless at the coming of our Lord Jesus Christ."*[18] Think about the blameless new life in our spirit, soul, and body. Accept the fact that your old life is dead and rejoice in your new life in Christ.

"It is because of him that you are in Christ Jesus."[19] God Himself, in a sovereign act, put us in Christ when we

accept Him as our Savior and become born again. Our spirit is merged and placed within the Spirit of Christ, which is merged with Father and the Holy Spirit.

Paul wrote, *"Don't you know that you yourselves are God's temple and that God's Spirit lives in you?"*[20] We are in God and God is in us because we are merged in the Spirit with Them. Paul taught the church in Galatia, *"You are all sons of God through faith in Christ Jesus, for all of you who were baptized into Christ have clothed yourselves with Christ."*[21] And, *"I have been crucified with Christ and I no longer live, but Christ lives in me. The life I live in the body, I live by faith in the Son of God, who loved me and gave himself for me."*[22] So God now reveals this mystery of the gospel, hidden from ages past, to mankind. Apostle Paul wrote extensively about the mystery, and its thread is woven throughout his Epistles in the New Testament of the Bible.

If you truly desire to walk in a new level of spirituality, then search out the "In Christ" message. Survey the verses in the Bible that include the words: in Christ, in Him, through Christ, etc. Then ask the Holy Spirit to give you the revelation of Christ in you and you in Him.

To understand and receive the revelation of who you are in Christ is a life-changing experience of the utmost importance. I'll never forget the day I received the revelation that Christ lives in me, and not just as a speck way down deep in my heart. But as I put Him on, He puts me on. His hands are in my hands. His feet are in my feet.

When I put my hand on someone in prayer and say, "In Jesus' name be healed," it isn't my hand that is significant, but it is the hand of the Lord Jesus within my hand. That is why we pray in His name. We are not using His name as a magic incantation, but we are letting all the forces of the enemy know that it is Christ in us who is praying and healing through us. It is His power, His ability, and His life—not ours. We are only vessels of the Lord.

This being the case, it is only proper to yield to the Spirit and allow Him to speak through us. So remember Jesus' words, *"For where two or three come together in my name, there am I with them."*[23] When we fellowship with Him in the Spirit, He will not only speak to us individually, but through one of us to the other. So when you come together, give Him a chance to speak to you through the Holy Spirit. Wait upon the Lord. Relax and let Him use you to speak to one another.

There is no arrogance or pride in us because of this relationship, but only sincere humility. No, we are not worthy, but His love and grace will flood us when we yield ourselves to Him. You see, He really desires a close intimate relationship with His children. Remember the words of Lord Jesus as recorded in the Bible:

> *...I pray also for those who will believe in me through their message, that all of them may be one, Father, just as you are in me and I am in you. May they also be in us so that the world may believe that you have sent me. I have given them the glory that you gave me, that they may be one as we are one: I in them and you in me. ... Father, I want those you have given me to be with me where I am, and to see my glory, the glory you have given me because you loved me before the creation of the world. ...I have made you known to them, and will continue to make you known in order that the love you have for me may be in them and that I myself may be in them.*[24]

So, dear reader, you see that Lord Jesus prayed to Father for us to have the relationship that Adam lost in the Garden restored to us. Seek Him. He can be found! You were made to be nothing less than a container, able to hold the very life of God Himself within you, enabling you to walk in the glory with Them where they are! That is our eternal destiny.

Our destiny is to be in Christ, and through Him, in Father. All that God is, all that They have, is open to us. No, we will never be gods ourselves, but we have been made to walk in the same benefits, the same life, and to be part of the same things that They, Father, Lord Jesus, and the Holy Spirit are.

All things were done, not just to forgive our sin but also to give us life! Their very life resides within us as believers. Don't focus on your weaknesses, for as long as you are in your body, you'll have weaknesses. But focus on the life God has given you!

The life God has given is far more able to keep you than anything the devil can throw at you. He is no match for the life in you. The life in you opens you up to God, His wisdom, and His revelation. God has given us a spiritual gift. He has shown us His kingdom. The next great awakening will be living out of the kingdom of God, living out of heaven. Through our relationship in Christ we not only have eternal life but we have the ability to live out of that eternity right now. We don't have to wait to die to go to heaven; we can live out of the kingdom here and now through Christ.

It is our identification with Christ—who and where we are in Him—that ties it all together and makes it all possible. The next great spiritual frontier, this next great awakening, will be the one that prepares the Church for the rapture. Pray that the Lord opens your spiritual eyes, so that you might begin to see and live out of the kingdom of heaven now. He is coming for those who are watching and waiting.

Praise God!

Chapter 7

Effective Prayer

So much has been written and taught about prayer. We have the Lord's Prayer, the official prayer of the Church on earth. We have bedtime prayers for the children, prayers of grace over dinner, prayers of thanks on Thanksgiving Day, prayers of comfort at funerals, prayers of hope at weddings, and prayers of dedication for babies. We have the "official" prayers down pat, but what about the everyday prayers of praise and fellowship with Father, Lord Jesus, and the Holy Spirit?

How does our prayer life measure up? Do we even have one? Does prayer become drudgery after ten minutes, when there is nothing left to say? Does your mind wander and your prayer time become a worrisome time with the cares of life dominating your thoughts? If so, then you are like many Christians in this busy world in which we live.

Well, what if I told you that there is a way to pray that will result in your walking in victory, always overcoming? A way that makes prayer fun, easy, and something you can't wait to do. I will show you how to take the drudgery out of prayer and turn it into a time of joy and fellowship with the Lord.

God's Word tells us that, *"The prayer of a righteous*

man is powerful and effective."[1] So we see by this Scripture, a truth. In order to be powerful and effective in prayer, we must be righteous. How do we know if we are righteous? Easy answer: are your prayers powerful and effective? If not, this chapter will show you how. If so, then great! This chapter will help you achieve a new level in Christ.

Before we can go further, we must examine ourselves. As we study what makes us who we are, we find that we are a spirit who possesses a soul and lives in a body. Apostle Paul wrote, *"May God himself, the God of peace, sanctify you through and through. May your whole spirit, soul and body be kept blameless at the coming of our Lord Jesus Christ."[2]*

He taught that we should be knowledgeable about ourselves. He wrote, *"That each of you should learn to control his own body in a way that is holy and honorable."[3]*

Spirit, Soul, and Body

Each person is made up of three parts: spirit, soul, and body. Our body is the part of us that enables us to experience this world. Our soul is the part of us that enables self-consciousness. And our spirit enables us to communicate into the realm of the Spirit, the realm of God.

"Don't you know that you yourselves are God's temple and that God's Spirit lives in you?"[4] The temple that was in Jerusalem as well as the temple in heaven is composed of three parts. First is the outer court, where all were permitted to enter. Then there's the Holy Place, where only the priests were permitted to enter. And finally the Holy of Holies, where God dwells and only the high priest was permitted to enter.

We, God's temple, also are made up of three parts. Our body, like the outer court is visible to all. It's open to the world. Our soul, like the Holy Place, is the inner part of our temple, not open to the public. It represents our inner life that is personal and exclusively private. And our spirit, like the Holy of Holies is where we are joined to God, the secret place of the Most High.

Communication from the world comes to our body, then to our soul, and then finally our spirit. Communication from God comes to our spirit, then to our soul, then finally to our body. So you see, our soul joins the body and spirit together. This will lead to a battle for dominion over our soul between our spirit and the body. It is of the utmost importance that we get a revelation of our spirit and understand its importance, because it is through our spirit that we communicate with God. *"For the word of God is living and active. Sharper than any double-edged sword, it penetrates even to dividing soul and spirit, joints and marrow."*[5] This Scripture confirms the separation of our spirit and soul. They are not one and the same. Each part of our tri-part being has faculties, which operates and constitutes the makeup of our person. In order to effectively understand each part, we must examine each faculty.

Spirit

Our spirit enables us to connect to the realm of God. *"God is spirit, and his worshipers must worship in spirit and in truth."*[6] Some teach that the body is evil, the spirit is infallible, and the soul is a pliable servant. That is not quite right. The spirit of a man is fallible. If it weren't, no one could ever renounce God. Even Granddaddy Adam couldn't have fallen. So let's look at the faculties of our spirit.

Intuition – Our intuition is the act or process of coming to direct knowledge or certainty without reasoning or innate knowledge. In other words, you just know. *"Immediately Jesus knew in his spirit that this was what they were thinking in their hearts."*[7] This is an example of the intuition of Jesus. He just knew. When your intuition is in tune with God, you intuitively hear His word and follow Him.

However, the intuition, even in redeemed man, is

capable of following a devil as well. Many have done so. In this liberal church climate in which we live, even some leaders have fallen very hard because they thought that their spirit and they themselves were infallible. Not keeping their guard up, they fell prey to doctrines of devils…and were destroyed by deceiving spirits.

The intuition is capable of hearing the voice of the Lord, and the voice of devils, angels of light, all in the spiritual realm. So then how can we distinguish between the two? We do it by staying close to the Lord in prayer. God's gifts are without repentance. In other words, God gives us gifts that He doesn't take back.

But many of His servants who operate in the spiritual gifts don't pray. They don't really know Him, and they can't possibly know Lord Jesus and Father if they don't spend enough time in prayer to know Them personally. So the enemy sets them up and knocks them down. But it doesn't have to be that way. An intuition in line with God will prevent defeat.

Communion – The second faculty of our spirit is our communion. This is the sharing of something in the spirit, an intimate fellowship with the Lord. Paul wrote, *"The communion of the Holy Spirit be with you all."*[8] Sometimes when you praise and worship the Lord in a church service, you find yourself in a higher form of praise in your spirit. It's like the clouds have rolled back and heaven itself is opened to you. It comes from deep within you. That is the communion faculty of your spirit connected to God. But again, if you don't stay clean before the Lord, your spirit could fall into communion with the enemy. Some preachers are having communion with devils and think they are having it with the Lord. I've seen it!

Conscience – The third faculty of our spirit is our conscience. This is the consciousness of moral right and wrong on our own acts and motives. The Bible says, *"Let us *draw near to God with a sincere heart in full assurance of faith, having our hearts sprinkled to cleanse us from a guilty conscience."*[9] This faculty guides toward right and away from wrong. However, the conscience can be defiled and seared. When our conscience is filled with guilt, we lose faith. Our conscience knows that we are guilty and relays to our brain that we really don't deserve to have our prayer answered, or to have any communication with God. It's like pouring clean water through a dirty filter. What you get is polluted water. Our conscience is like that polluted filter when it is filled with guilt and shame. It skews our communications with the Lord and hinders our faith. We are told in the Bible, *"How much more, then, will the blood of Christ...cleanse our consciences from acts that lead to death."*[10]

Soul

The second part of our tri-part being is the soul. The essence of an individual life is the soul. Our soul is who we are. As God breathes life into an unborn child at conception, He makes the child a living soul. Like the spirit, there are faculties of the soul.

Mind – The first faculty of the soul is the mind. It's the part of us that feels, thinks, and perceives. Jesus said, *"Love the Lord your God with all your heart and with all your soul and with all your mind."*[11] Our reason and intellect rests in our mind.

Will – The second faculty of our soul is our will. This can be described as our desire, determination, volition, and our power of controlling our actions. The control of our will must be totally submitted to God.

Emotions – The third faculty of our soul is our emotions. These can be described as deep feelings. An example of this is found in the Psalms, *"My soul yearns, and even faints, for the courts of the Lord; my heart and my flesh cry out* *for the living God."*[12] Our affections, desire, love, hate, and despair are only some of the manifestations of our emotions. Some people are more emotional than others, but we all have emotions that must be submitted to God.

Body

The third part of our tri-part being is our body. Natural man without God is a man of senses who relates only to this world. Before Adam's fall, he was of light and glory. Adam operated out of his spirit, to his soul, and then to his body. But since the fall of Adam, man operates in the flesh in a combination of soul and body, which work together. Man relates and communicates with the natural world through his five senses: sight, hearing, taste, touch, and smell.

Sight – To see or behold.

Hearing – The act or power of perceiving sound.

Taste – To ascertain the flavor of by taking a small quantity into the mouth.

Touch – To bring a body part into contact with something so as to feel.

Smell – To perceive an aroma by inhaling through the nose.

So here we are with these three wonderful parts of ourselves and these eleven faculties, which were originally designed by God to work in unity. We were meant to live out of the Spirit realm and fellowship with God, as well as the earthly realm where we fellowship with each other.

This is the complete person whom God created. It is easy to see how that after the fall, with our spirits dead to God, our soul and body took over and made the flesh our world. We can better understand the Scripture that says, *"For the sinful nature desires what is contrary to the Spirit, and the Spirit what is contrary to the sinful nature. They are in conflict with each other, so that you do not do what you want."*[13]

Even dedicated Christians struggle with sin in some part of their tri-part being, so it is no wonder they struggle to achieve effective prayer. But there is a way. We must take up our cross, that is, our part of His cross, and follow Him. Jesus is the way. We must follow in His steps, in Him.

A Planned Course

What athlete doesn't prepare before the great event? They punish their bodies in order to be in shape and prepared for the challenge ahead. So it is with us in prayer. Just as there are a variety of sporting events one might prepare for, there are a variety of prayer challenges for which to prepare.

If we are about to pray in intercession for others, we must prepare. Maybe we are going into spiritual warfare with lives hanging in the balance. Well, we had better be prepared. Or suppose we just want to spend time with the Lord in fellowship? Certainly that requires preparation as well.

Several years ago I had the privilege of hearing Pastor David Paul Yonggi Cho, pastor of the world's largest church, located in South Korea, speak in a meeting in Virginia. It was a thrill to shake his hand afterward and exchange pleasantries. But the most incredible thing was that he taught a very subtle version of the steps to effective prayer that I am about to share with you.

He spoke about approaching prayer as a discipline, somewhat similar to a runner as he approaches his regimen of running. He said, "Use your imagination. Prayer is like jogging. If you get up and jog one morning, and then you don't jog for a day or two, and then you jog for a few minutes the next morning, then you're not a disciplined jogger. Prayer is like that. If you get up and pray one morning, then go a few days and don't pray, then you are not a disciplined pray-er. In prayer you need to go places. There is a fifteen-minute jog, or prayer, a thirty-minute jog, or prayer, and a one-hour marathon jog, or prayer."

He continued, "When you are jogging, you run down a road and get to one corner and turn, then you get to a tree and turn. There are certain landmarks, certain places that you go when you jog, especially when you jog every day and are disciplined to do it. The same is true in prayer. We know that the temple described in the Old Testament is a representation of the temple in heaven, and a foreshadowing of Christ. Imagine yourself going to the temple." This was incredible because this is what I was taught by the Lord. Nowhere had I heard even a hint of anything this close to how the Lord taught me to pray effectively.

Dr. Cho suggested establishing landmarks in prayer as a runner establishes landmarks in his running routine. The runner in training doesn't just start running without a plan or purpose. He knows where he is going and pushes himself to certain limits at specified boundaries, or landmarks, finishing one, and then moving on to the next. Likewise, we must have a plan, goals, and the discipline to achieve them.

I suppose I'll never know how deep into this Pastor Cho delves in his personal prayer life, but he touched on enough of it in his subtle way that I believe he's got it. The Lord taught me directly for three years, in prayer, visions, and the Word, and then many more years of practical use and experience before I was ready to share this way of effective prayer.

My heart rejoiced as the Spirit witnessed this confirmation from the man whom God used to build His largest church in the world. God brought Pastor Cho, a man for whom I already had great confidence and admiration, all the way around the world from Korea to Virginia Beach, and gave me confirmation in his message! Hallelujah! Now let us proceed.

Therefore, since we are surrounded by such a great cloud of witnesses, let us throw off everything that hinders and the sin that so easily entangles, and let us run with perseverance the race marked out for us.[14]

Chapter 8

The Steps

The Steps to Effective Prayer

Therefore, brothers, since we have confidence to enter the Most Holy Place by the blood of Jesus, by a new and living way opened for us through the curtain, that is, his body.[1]

The Blood of Jesus

We must see in ourselves the need to daily come to God, through the blood of Jesus, because of sin. We must repent for the acts of sin we commit. For every act of sin we know of, there are many that we don't know we have committed. Those sins must be addressed as well. We struggle with sin because we are in this sinful world. As bad as the sin we commit, is the effect it has on us. When we sin, we allow the force of sin inside us. The force of sin sets itself up inside us. That's why we have trouble praying. That's why we have trouble living for God. It's not just rebellion. If that were the case we wouldn't be troubled by it. The fact that it grieves us is proof that we don't want to sin or be controlled by our sin nature.

So if we're acting contrary to our own will, it is no longer us but sin that is inside us, controlling us, manipulating us. It's a force and a power, not just an act. So you see we're born again into the kingdom of God. How could we be the problem? No. It's not us! It's sin in us that's the problem. See the distinction? The blood of Jesus satisfies God. We must believe this and let it also satisfy us. *"For you know that it was not with perishable things such as silver or gold that you were redeemed from the empty way of life handed down to you from your forefathers, but with the precious blood of Christ, a lamb without blemish or defect."*[2] Never answer the accuser with good conduct and good works, but only with the blood of Jesus. Our faith in the blood of Jesus puts Satan to flight.

Pray, "Lord Jesus, I come to You through Your blood. I ask You to forgive me for any sin I have committed either known or unknown. I ask You to destroy the force of sin within me."

The blood of Jesus not only covers your sins, but it will destroy sin as a force in your life. Our prayers are ineffectual because we have to battle sin to get to God. Sometimes we live and pray more victoriously than at other times. We have been given the victorious life in Christ and can live in victory all the time if we will search ourselves and ask the Lord to cleanse every faculty in our tri-part being—spirit, soul, and body. Now pray for this deep cleansing.

Spirit

Pray, "Lord Jesus, forgive me for any sin, known or unknown, in my spirit's faculty of intuition. Destroy the force of sin, by Your blood, in my intuition." Immediately, something has happened. Your intuition is free from sin by the blood of Jesus. Nothing is now between your intuition and the Lord. Now pray the same again for your spiritual faculty of will, then emotions.

Pray, "Lord Jesus, forgive me for any sin, known or unknown, in my spirit's faculty of communion. Destroy the force of sin, by Your blood, in my communion." It's done! You're liberated already.

Pray, "Lord Jesus, forgive me for any sin, known or unknown, in my spirit's faculty of conscience. Destroy the force of sin, by Your blood, in my conscience." At this moment maybe you are sensing the freedom and liberation of your spirit. Your sin is not only covered, but sin, as a force, has been rooted out of your spirit.

Soul

Pray, "Lord Jesus, forgive me for any sin, known or unknown, in my soul's faculty of the mind. Destroy the force of sin, by Your blood, in my mind." Your mind is free!

Pray, "Lord Jesus, forgive me for any sin, known or unknown in my soul's faculty of my will. Destroy the force of sin, by Your blood, in my will." Your will is free from sin, unmarred, opened to Jesus.

Pray, "Lord Jesus, forgive me for any sin, known or unknown, in my soul's faculty of emotions. Destroy the force of sin, by Your blood, in my emotions." Your soul is now liberated, free to Jesus. Each step makes you freer than the step before. You can sense it. When you complete these steps, the rest of prayer is easy and very effective.

Body

The body is not just your flesh; it is your five physical senses. When you deal with your senses, you deal with the power of the body.

Pray, "Lord Jesus, forgive me for any sin, known or unknown, in my body's sense of sight. Destroy the force of sin, by Your blood, in my sight." Now pray again the same for each of your other senses: hearing, then taste, then touch, then smell. When you do this for the first time, it may take a little time as you pause at each step and allow the Holy Spirit to do His work in you. Some faculties of your tri-part being may need more time and cleansing than others. The next time you go through this, the dynamics change depending on the need in any given faculty. Be patient. Allow the Lord to do His work in you.

You are free because the blood of Jesus is more powerful than sin. It is sin that causes your mind to wander in prayer. Sin opposes Christ and keeps His Spirit from working in you. If you will start with this as you begin in prayer, you will be free. You will notice this freedom inside because there is nothing there opposing you. The force of sin is gone!

The Cross

For God was pleased to have all his fullness dwell in him, and through him to reconcile to himself all things, whether things on earth or things in heaven, by making peace through his blood, shed on the cross.[3]

We need the blood for forgiveness; we need the cross for deliverance. The blood deals with the sins, the cross deals with the sinner. The blood procures our pardon for what we have done; the cross procures our deliverance from what we are.

For we know that our old self was crucified with him so that the body of sin might be done away with, that we should no longer be slaves to sin—because anyone who has died has been freed from sin.[4]

The death of Christ was our death. Let us go back to the cross. Hear the wind blow. See Jesus hanging on the cross. Now see yourself hanging on the cross, in Christ, because that is what happened. You are crucified. You must confess, "I have been crucified with Christ."

You are not *trying* to be crucified, you *have been* crucified with Christ Jesus. It is not pleasant to be crucified. Ask the Holy Spirit to let you see yourself crucified with and in Christ Jesus. His death was our death. Natural man does not like to be crucified. It is uncomfortable. We were crucified on the cross in Him and we died in Him! Don't stop at the foot of the cross. As I said before, take up your cross, your part of His cross, and follow Him. Ask the Holy Spirit to work the death of Christ out in you—spirit, soul, and body, and every part of your tri-part being.

Spirit

Pray, "Lord Jesus, I give You my spirit's faculty of intuition, crucified on the cross in You." Now pray and submit your spirit's faculty of communion, then your conscience. You now see that your spirit has been crucified on the cross in Christ Jesus. You may already know this as doctrine, but now the Lord is making it real in your life. You are experiencing the reality of it.

Soul

Pray, "Lord Jesus, I give You my soul's faculty of my mind, crucified on the cross in You." Now pray and submit your soul's faculty of will, then your emotions. Your soul is there. You see it there, on the cross, in Christ.

Body

Pray, "Lord Jesus, I give You my body's sense of sight, crucified on the cross in You." Now pray and submit your body's senses of hearing, then your taste, then your touch, then smell. Yes this may be uncomfortable, but the Holy Spirit will take the natural man and put him on the cross. Why? We were crucified on the cross in Christ, and we died. We must allow the Holy Spirit to put to death each faculty of our tri-part being. We died in Christ on the cross. We must reckon ourselves dead. The pain and discomfort of the cross is now over—for we have died in Christ.

The Grave

Who qualifies for burial? The dead qualify for burial. What does a dead man feel? Nothing, a dead man feels nothing. Think about it. You feel dead, do you not? This is the power of Christ. It is His working. Not only did you die, you were buried. Imagine yourself in the tomb with Christ, dead, buried, lying on the slab, and wrapped in His grave clothes with Him, in Him. When He went into hell, you went with Him, in Him. So now, the Lord has taken care of sin, and taken care of you. Paul explains, *"Don't you know that all of us who were baptized into Christ Jesus were baptized into his death? We were therefore buried with Him through baptism into death in order that, just as Christ was raised from the dead through the glory of the Father, we too may live a new life."*[5]

Pray, "Lord Jesus, my spirit's faculties of intuition, communion, and conscience are dead in You. Your death is my death."

Pray, "Lord Jesus, my soul's faculties of mind, will, and emotions are dead in You. Your death is my death."

Pray, "Lord Jesus, my body's faculties of sight, hearing, taste, touch, and smell are dead in You. Your death is my death." God made an intimate union between Christ and us in His death, burial, and resurrection. At this point you may feel nothing. After all, you are dead. His death was your death.

Resurrection

If we have been united with Him like this in His death, we will certainly also be united with Him in His resurrection. For we know that our old self was crucified with Him so that the body of sin might be done away with, that we should no longer be slaves to sin—because anyone who has died has been freed from sin. Now if we died with Christ, we believe that we will also live with Him. For we know that since Christ was raised from the dead, He cannot die again; death no longer has mastery over Him. The death He died, He died to sin once for all; but the life He lives, He lives to God.

The apostle Paul wrote, *"In the same way, count yourselves dead to sin but alive to God in Christ Jesus."*[6] When Christ Jesus came out of the tomb, we all came out of the tomb in Him. His resurrection was our resurrection because He was raised for us. God, through the Holy Spirit, gave us life when Christ Jesus was given life. We enter into His death—His resurrection enters into us. Your natural life has now been changed, a new life, a divine life, has become yours. Again, we go down the list and ask the Lord to give our tri-part being resurrected life in Christ Jesus.

Spirit

Pray, "Lord Jesus, give me life in my spirit's faculty of intuition, in You." You should feel it come on like a light bulb—your spirit coming to life in Christ. Now continue to pray and ask for His life in your communion and then your conscience. Your spirit is now alive in Christ. It is more alive than ever before because sin is gone, and the old man, of who you were, is gone. Your spirit has perfect freedom and you should sense it. Again, we pray by faith.

Soul

Pray, "Lord Jesus, give me life in my soul's faculty of mind, in You." Then pray and ask for life in your soul's faculty of will and emotion. Your spirit and soul are now flooded with new life!

Body

Pray, "Lord Jesus, give me life in my body's sense of sight, in You." Next continue by praying for life, His life, in your other senses of hearing, then taste, then touch, then smell. You now feel alive in Christ—spirit, soul, and body! Notice the difference in how you felt with sin alive inside versus now, with sin and the force of sin gone, with the old you crucified. You are now walking in perfect unity—spirit, soul, and body—in the life of Christ Jesus. What you feel is His very life coursing through you!

Chapter 9

Follow Boldly into Heaven

We recall from the book of Genesis the story of how God called Abraham from his life and the land of his Fathers to a new life of faith and to a land of his own. God delivered, a nation was born, and Abraham was blessed. Abraham followed boldly, and now we have the opportunity to follow boldly as well, into a relationship, a fellowship in the Spirit.

Will we follow Christ, the Holy Spirit and Father? God's Word says that we may *"come boldly unto the throne of grace."*[1] Does that mean every believer? Yes. If God's throne is open to us, doesn't it make sense that all of heaven is also open to us? If He would open up His very throne room, then wouldn't He also open the river of life to us, or the heavenly city and other places in the heavenly realm as well? We have the right to go there now. We don't have to wait. We can go there every day. It's part of our heritage.

Why should we have to die physically to go there? Why should we have to undergo the turmoil of this world without it? We need heaven now more than we'll need it then. We need a spiritual journey, a trip. Jesus didn't come out of the tomb and just speak to His disciples. He went to the Father. And He'll take our spirits there also.

Pray, "Father, in Jesus' name, lead me where You want

me to go. Holy Spirit, take control of my Spirit and help me to follow Jesus into fellowship with You. Lord Jesus, I submit my will to You. I'm alive in You. I have been raised and seated in heavenly places in You."

Dear reader, I pray your spiritual eyes be opened to see the realm of heaven we have in Christ Jesus. If you don't see yet, it's all right. Your spirit sees.

Altar

In heaven is the original altar and temple from which God gave Moses the specifications to duplicate on earth. First was the tabernacle in the wilderness, then the actual temple in Jerusalem. The one in heaven is the temple not made with hands, but made by God.

Here, in the Spirit on the altar in heaven, we offer ourselves as living sacrifices to God, which is our reasonable service. People have taken "offering ourselves as living sacrifices" to mean to deny ourselves. No! A living sacrifice is something that is alive, not dead. You see, He doesn't need a natural carnal man as a living sacrifice. He can't do anything with him. But since you have gone through these steps, you have crucified the natural, done away with the sin inside, and are filled with the life of Christ.

Now you are alive to God and are a clean, pure sacrifice, holy to the Lord, which He can use. Are you willing to be sacrificed? *"I beseech you therefore, brethren, by the mercies of God, that ye present your bodies a living sacrifice, holy, acceptable unto God, which is your reasonable service."*[2]

In your mind and spirit, lay yourself upon the altar in heaven. Feel the blood of Jesus cover you as you present yourself, your clean, pure self to God. This whole process is very personal. It is personal to me; and as you do this, it will be personal and precious to you as well. Know that it is most precious to the Lord.

Pray, "Lord Jesus, I present myself a living sacrifice and lay upon the altar in heaven. Let my spirit, soul, and body be covered in Your blood. Let the fire of the Holy Spirit accept this sacrifice in union with You."

Spirit

Pray, "Lord Jesus, I give You my spirit's faculty of intuition, as a living sacrifice." Next pray and offer Him your spirit's faculty of communion, then your conscience.

Soul

Pray, "Lord Jesus, I give you my soul's faculty of mind, as a living sacrifice." Next pray and offer Him your soul's faculty of will, then your emotions.

Body

Pray, "Lord Jesus, I give You my body's sense of sight, as a living sacrifice." Now pray and offer Him your body's senses of hearing, then your taste, then your touch, then your smell. Do you not feel it? Isn't the glory getting deeper? As the Holy Spirit blesses you in these steps, you will experience the glory of God in a deeper way. And you can do this every day as you prepare yourself for prayer and fellowship with God. Praise God!

Pray, "Lord Jesus, I have given you every part of me—spirit, soul, and body. May Your blood on this altar cover me and the Holy Spirit seal me with His fire." As you lay on the altar, the fire of the Holy Spirit descends upon you. His presence overshadows you as He accepts your sacrifice. When you come off the altar, like me, you can see Christ in the mirror as your reflection. Your oneness and identity with Him are stronger than ever.

Sea of Glass

In heaven, just beyond the altar to the left of the temple sits the sea of glass: *"And I saw what looked like a sea of glass mixed with fire."*[3] The Old Testament tells of a giant bowl for water, which was made to cleanse and purify the priests. This was called the laver, or the sea. It represented on earth, the sea of glass in heaven. The sea comes out of the throne of God and is very holy. It is a place of sanctification upon which the very holiness of God rests. We are free to go over and touch, walk, or lay upon it. It is solid like a glass floor; and like the holiness of the Lord, it stretches out into the horizon like a never-ending sea. Imagine yourself stretched out lying upon it. You have the right to do this. It doesn't matter if you see it or not. This is not about visions, for your spirit can see it even if you don't right now. This is a point of contact between you and God's holiness. Sanctification is a gift. Receive it.

Spirit

Pray, "Lord Jesus, as I lay upon the sea of glass, I give You my spirit's faculty of intuition. Sanctify it, make it holy." There, it just happened! Pray and offer your faculties of communion and conscience upon the sea of glass.

Soul

Pray, "Lord Jesus, as I lay upon the sea of glass, I give You my soul's faculty of mind. Sanctify it, make it holy." Pray and offer your soul's faculty of will and then your emotions to be sanctified upon the sea of glass.

Body

Pray, "Lord Jesus, as I lay upon the sea of glass, I give You my body's sense of sight. Sanctify it, make it holy." Now pray and offer your body's senses of hearing, then your taste, then your touch, then smell. Now your spirit, soul, and body are truly holy in a new and marvelous way. Feel the joy that this brings. Hallelujah! Now you know why the apostles prayed so much. To follow the way of Christ takes some time. Some days it takes longer than others, but it is surely worth it. In the midst of your joy, understand why you feel it. Have you ever felt so clean? Have you ever felt so pure and holy?

Do you see how each step builds upon the other? You are now a vessel that has died to sin, died to self, rose in newness of life, given to the Lord Jesus as a living sacrifice, sanctified holy, and ready for a fresh infilling of the Holy Spirit. Remember the prayer of the apostle Paul: *"May God himself, the God of peace, sanctify you through and through. May your whole spirit, soul and body be kept blameless at the coming of our Lord Jesus Christ."*[4]

The Lamp Stand

Now you are ready for the most glorious of all. You were made for union with God, the Three. That's what it's all about. So we leave the sea of glass in heaven, and walk up the steps of the temple and enter in. Entering the Holy Place, we find it dark inside, but for the light of the seven candlesticks on the left side of the room. There we find the precious Holy Spirit. He is in the midst of the flames, above and about the candlesticks.

Apostle John wrote about the lampstands in the temple in heaven: *"I turned around to see the voice that was speaking to me. And when I turned I saw seven golden lampstands."*[5] See the loveliness of the Holy Spirit. As you stand before the lamp stand, ask Him for a fresh infilling into your spirit, soul, and body.

Pray, "Holy Spirit, fill my spirit, soul, and body with Your fire and give me a revelation of You and I joined together in union, as one." As the Holy Spirit floods you, sense how your spirit, soul, and body are functioning together, none opposing the other. Your mind is not wandering way over there while your body fidgets uncomfortably. No, your whole being is working in harmony as God created you to be. Feel the Holy Spirit in union within you.

It is a fallacy to think that you receive the baptism of the Holy Spirit one time and that's the end of it. No, we need a constant refilling of the Spirit, so come to Him daily and ask Him to fill you and give you a revelation of His presence and union with you. Soak Him in like a sponge.

Table of Shewbread

On the opposite side of the room sits a table upon which are loaves of bread and a carafe of wine. The Bible speaks of this, *"Solomon also made all the furnishings that were in the Lord's temple: the golden altar, the golden table on which was the bread of the Presence."*[6] Jesus is the living Word, the Bread of Life. At the table of shewbread we put on Christ and gain fresh revelation about the Living Word. In the Spirit, we can take the bread from the table, consume it, and drink of the wine. He will give you a revelation of Himself and your union together as you receive communion in the heavenly temple.

Pray, "Lord Jesus, as I eat of the bread and drink of the wine I ask You to give me a fresh revelation of our union together in my spirit, soul, and body. Let You, me, and the Holy Spirit be joined as one." Hallelujah! What power! What completeness and joy! People who do this every day conquer devils. This is truly the bread of Your presence precious Lord!

Altar of Incense

One of my favorite spots in heaven is standing at the altar of incense with Lord Jesus and interceding in prayer to the Father:

> *This is the confidence we have in approaching God: that if we ask anything according to his will, he hears us. And if we know that he*

hears us—whatever we ask—we know that we have what we asked of him.[7]

Therefore, since we have a great high priest who has gone through the heavens, Jesus the Son of God, let us hold firmly to the faith we profess.[8]

On this waist-high altar, incense burns, which causes smoke to rise and fill the Holy Place, the prayers of the saints and sinners alike come up through the altar and mingle with the smoke. They enter the atmosphere with the voice of many waters, indistinguishable to the normal human ear, but the Lord hears and understands them all. When you serve as priest with Him, He will allow you to hear certain prayers in order to join in intercession through Him, to the Father. When you understand a request, you pray to the Father. When you petition the Father from here, through Christ, you have no doubt in your mind that He hears you. Every petition, every request is heard and given full attention and consideration by the Father. Of this you have full confidence.

Sometimes you just stand and observe the Lord performing His duties as the great High Priest interceding for mankind to the Father. At other times, He enjoys you joining Him in intercession. Either way, it is the thrill of a lifetime.

Pray, "Lord Jesus, I love to intercede in prayer with You. Let every faculty of my spirit, soul, and body be in tune with You as we minister before Father together."

The Ark

We read about the Ark of the Covenant in the Bible.[9] The earthly ark has slipped through history and its current location is unknown. Did God transport it to heaven?

Then God's temple in heaven was opened, and within his temple was seen the ark of his covenant. And there came flashes of lightning, rumblings, peals of thunder, an earthquake and a great hailstorm.[10]

Fellowship in the Spirit

If you walk a few steps past the altar of incense in the Holy Place, you'll enter the throne room of God, which corresponds to the Holy of Holies in the earthly temple. Just inside the throne room is the ark. We are always welcome to enter the throne room. The ark on earth contained the stone tablets of the Ten Commandments, a pot of manna from the wilderness, and Aaron's rod that budded. The ark in heaven, as John explained, contains flashes of lightning, rumblings, and peals of thunder, an earthquake and a great hailstorm. It contains the very power and glory of God.

Move quietly toward the ark in union with Lord Jesus and the Holy Spirit. Father will meet you there. Prepare to move to a new level of spiritual intensity. When you add union with the Father with Lord Jesus and the Holy Spirit, you have the one God, Yahweh, come alive in you. They will give you a revelation of union with Them on the highest level.

Pray, "Holy Father, we stand in union with the Spirit and the Son asking You for a divine audience in the Holy of Holies that we might be in union with You." He bids us come and we walk to the ark. We walk in the light as He is in the light. We are joined in union with our Father and the Son and the Spirit. We are now in the light. If your spiritual eyes are open, you see a bright white light, which is union with Them.

This is why They did what They did. This is why Jesus died, to achieve this union with you. Your spirit and Their Spirits all dissolving one into the other, like butter in a hot skillet, melting together into one in union. There's power in union. In union entwined with Them, you are so lost in Them that you couldn't get out if They didn't help you. Isn't it glorious to know that you can do this every day? It gets better. We're going through the tri-part being again. But now, you understand, it is no longer Father, Lord Jesus, and Holy Spirit, it is the one triune God, Yahweh. Now you understand how

They are three and how They are one. We may address Them as God or Yahweh. Either name means the Three in total unity as One.

Spirit

Pray, "Yahweh, I give You my intuition. Open my spirit's intuition to Your light." There it goes! Your intuition is flooded with light! Continue your prayer and give Him your spirit's faculty of communion and then your conscience, opening them to His light. Now your spirit is in total union with Them. When the apostle said to walk in the light, he literally meant to walk in the light, but more about that later. This is God on the highest level. The light is open to you for you belong to Them, and They want to share it with you. It's the highest fellowship possible.

Soul

Pray, "Yahweh, I give You my mind. Open my soul's mind to Your light." Now give Him your soul's faculty of will, and then your emotions. See how your soul is flooded with light. What glory!

Body

Pray, "Yahweh, I give You my sight. Open my body's sense of sight to Your light." Next give Him your body's faculty of hearing, then your taste, then your touch, and then your smell. At any time you can speak with Them and ask for any spiritual gift. Ask Them to impart Their attributes to you: love, peace, joy, kindness, etc. They will guide you as you are merged with them in the Spirit. When They release you from this state, you are free to spend time in praise and worship in the throne room.

Throne Room

> *After this I looked and there before me was a great multitude that no one could count, from every nation, tribe, people and language, standing before the throne and in front of the Lamb. They were wearing white robes and were holding palm branches in their hands. And they cried out in a loud voice: "Salvation belongs to our God, who sits on the throne and to the Lamb."[11]*

It's a joy to worship God in the throne room with the multitudes of the saints. This is your privilege and honor. Enjoy!

The Armor

Now it's time to suit up for spiritual warfare. Apostle Paul described the preparation process this way:

> *Put on the full armor of God so that you can take your stand against the devil's schemes. For our struggle is not against flesh and blood, but against the rulers, against the authorities, against the powers of this dark world and against the spiritual forces of evil in the heavenly realms. Therefore put on the full armor of God, so that when the day of evil comes, you may be able to stand your ground, and after you have done everything, to stand. Stand firm then, with the belt of truth buckled around your waist, with the breastplate of righteousness in place, and with your feet fitted with the readiness that comes from the gospel of peace. In addition to all this, take up the shield of faith, with which you can extinguish all the flaming arrows of the evil one. Take the helmet of salvation and the sword of the Spirit, which is the word of God. And pray in the Spirit on all occasions with all kinds of prayers and requests. With this in mind, be alert and always keep on praying for all the saints.[12]*

Remember that this is His armor, not ours. We are one with Him and so His armor permeates us. When the enemy sees us, he thinks God is inside because it's His armor. The armor and what it represents are attributes of God. Put Him on.

Become like Him.

Now you are ready to pray and intercede if the Lord is calling you to do so. There's nothing between you and Them; you have clear vision and can pray in His power in union with Him. It's all about union with Them and Them reproducing Themselves in you. Do these steps daily and you will walk in power and overcome the enemy. If you let time elapse, it takes more time to get back in spiritual shape.

Now when you are done with intercession and worship in the temple, a great treat is in store…heaven. That's right; you may walk right out of the throne room and take a stroll through heaven. The Spirit will lead you. I pray that your spiritual eyes will be opened right now in the name of Jesus!

Chapter 10

Heaven

Paul's prayer to the Ephesians expressed his desire for them to see in the Spirit and experience the heavenly realm. He wrote, *"I pray also that the eyes of your heart may be enlightened in order that you may know the hope to which he has called you, the riches of his glorious inheritance in the saints."*[1] This is my desire for you as well. I can only begin to describe the wonders and marvelous glory that is heaven. But I'll try.

The first thing you notice about heaven is the atmosphere. The air is so fresh! You breathe deeply to get as much air into your lungs as possible, and then you continue to breathe in more. You want the air to fill every pore in the deepest recesses of your lungs, somehow purging the air of earth, with all its impurities, out of your being. Completely filled with the air of heaven, you hold your breath as long as you can, not wanting to expel the most pure, fresh air you have ever breathed.

There is an aroma in the air. It's a mixture of fragrance unlike anything earthly. The flowers, grass, trees, river, fruit, leaves, and various plants combine into an aroma that is delicious to smell. I could stand still and breathe this forever! The atmosphere, like everything else in heaven, is satisfying, yet leaves you wanting more.

> *Your plants are an orchard of pomegranates with choice fruits, with henna and nard, nard and saffron, calamus and cinnamon, with every kind of incense tree, with myrrh and aloes and all the finest spices. You are a garden fountain, a well of flowing water streaming down....*[2]

A Celebration in Heaven

People are gathered on both sides of Main Street in heaven today. The street is made of pure, solid gold. It is so pure that it is almost transparent. Looking at it, you can see into it. There are curbs on each side made of diamonds. Yet, it looks like one solid length of diamond that lines the curb of the road, not individual diamonds encrusted into the curb. There is anticipation in the crowd as they wait. Joy and excitement, intertwined with patient calm, fills the air. People are gathered as far as I can see in both directions.

Coming down the street from my left is the procession. It's Jesus! He is walking in front of a group of people. He has the biggest and most beautiful smile on His face! I have to laugh! There is so much joy in my heart from just seeing Him. He looks so happy!

I do not recognize the people with Jesus at first, but the Spirit lets me know who they are. The first group of people walking with Him, beside and behind Him, is His earthly family, friends, and followers.

That is, His disciples, mother Mary, father Joseph, brothers, and other family and close friends. John the Baptist and the apostle Paul are also there.

Immediately behind them are angels. I might add that these are not just any angels, but angels who had played a part in the Lord's earthly life. These were mentioned in the Bible, including the one who told Mary that she would conceive, the choir that proclaimed His birth, and the angel who told His disciples that He would come again, as He ascended. They are all here. The patriarchs of the Bible, His entire family line back to Adam, follow them!

It is one glorious party! People are dancing in the streets, singing and shouting praises to them, praying and worshipping Him and Father. Father isn't in the procession, but the procession began in Father's presence in the temple, before the throne. As Jesus and the rest of the procession passes, those on the sides of the street fall in behind them and continue with them through the city. There are throngs of people. I can hear them on the side, waiting with anticipation saying, "Here comes the Lord!" And, "Look! There He is!" Then they shout and praise Him as He passes by.

Although He is walking, and there are untold multitudes of people along the procession route, He seems to smile and make eye contact with every single person in the crowd as He passes by. The joy of this is indescribable! This is a true triumphal entry! This entry into the city of God, in heaven, by Jesus the Savior, and Lord of all! Hallelujah!

> *Praise the LORD. Sing to the LORD a new song, his praise in the assembly of the saints. Let Israel rejoice in their Maker; let the people of Zion be glad in their King. Let them praise his name with dancing and make music to him with tambourine and harp. For the LORD takes delight in his people....*[3]

The River of Joy

In the Spirit, I had been in the forest of God resting after having spent time with the Lord. Sitting comfortably on a wall of stone, I think to myself that this is a good place to rest for a while. I'll stay here for a time and enjoy myself. I'll reflect on the events of the day and what they all mean. As I lean back on my hands and begin what I think is going to be a time of reflection, an angel appears on my right. I jump to my feet and with my heart in my throat say, "Hello."

He says, "Greetings. We must go."

Now, I won't say he is intimidating, his being nine feet tall and mighty, but his appearance and demeanor causes me to comply immediately. I say, "Sure, after you."

He nods slightly toward me, then turns and walks into the clearing toward a direction I have not been. I think to myself, *This is nice,* then hurry to catch up. The angel leads me from the clearing, through the forest to the other side and then we stop. We are at the edge of the forest. I can see that he is going no farther as he turns sideways and stretches out his right hand, directing me to continue on. I stop in front of him, look up into his face, and say, "Thank you."

He says, "Surely."

I ask if I would ever see him again, and he replies, "No, I don't think so."

I bid him farewell and walk on out of the forest. As I step out, it is as if I have stepped through a curtain into another realm. I feel different! I feel light as a feather. I'm not floating, but it sure seems like I could. The air is so fresh! A feeling of euphoria comes over me from my head down to my feet like a wave. Then, wave after wave comes over me. I open my mouth to praise the Lord, but I am so overcome with this euphoric feeling that no sound, no words will come out of my mouth. I just breathe deep breaths and stand here.

The smile on my face has to be the biggest I've ever had because this feeling is joy magnified! The waves of euphoria don't stop; they just run together and become joy unspeakable! Normally we feel joy when something good happens to us, but this joy is not in response to something good happening to me. Pure joy is what is happening to me. All my emotions are becoming joyful. My total existence is joyous! Joy is birthed inside my being and is working its way out of me by soaking itself out through every pore, and every molecule of my being.

Every gospel song I have ever heard about joy comes to mind, and though I enjoy them, they are pitifully inappropriate to express this feeling that I have. I search my mind for an explanation, but resign myself to accept the fact that this joy is unexplainable, and unspeakable.

The River Is Wide

After some time, I become more comfortable with this new existence. I suddenly realize that my eyes have been closed, so I open them. Looking down at my feet, I realize I am standing on water! Whoa! What is this! It feels solid, like ground, but it is water! I am not sinking, yet I am not floating. I lift my right leg slowly to take a step and I definitely feel gravity, however, I am lighter. I can move almost effortlessly. This is great! Waves of joy still flow over me as I begin to walk. Though I don't see anybody, I don't feel alone. I feel as safe and secure as I would in my own bed.

Looking around, it appears to me that I am in the middle, no, on the middle of a great river. Looking down, I see that the river is moving slightly to my right, but I am not being moved. I am walking straight across toward the other side. I can see a shore in the distance, but nothing more. Though I am enjoying the euphoric feelings, I find myself thinking of my past. Every thought is a pleasant one. I remember faces I haven't thought of in years. Family I only saw as a baby, or as a small child, who have gone on to be with the Lord, come to mind.

I remember the kind words, smiling faces, and expressions of love. I am remembering things I have never thought of since they happened. Ha! Any kind word or expression anyone has ever given me is coming back to my remembrance! It is wonderful! I feel so loved! It's as if the whole world loved me! Not one negative thought exists in my remembrance! Only love, peace, and joy remain!

A huge wave of joy comes over me, and I feel every hug that has ever been given to me in my whole life, all at the same time! Standing here and not moving, I wrap my arms around myself. With my head back and my mouth open breathing deeply, I feel every hug I've ever received, from the first one my mother gave me as a newborn baby, every family hug growing up, my friends, my wife, my child, my brothers and sisters at church, to God's hugs. I am reliving them all! What a feeling! What joy!

As this subsides, I stretched the biggest stretch I ever have. I take a few steps toward the shore, and then I hear it. I hear my mother's voice. It is the voice of my earliest memory. It is the first voice I remember as a baby saying the simple words, "I love you." I stop in my "wet" tracks again and remember. First my mother, then my father said, "Son, I love you." I could hear their voices. Now the memory of voices long forgotten echo in my mind and in my heart, "I love you."

Every person who ever uttered those words to me is coming back to my remembrance, and the joy I feel explodes in my heart. Tears of joy stream from my eyes as I speak back to my memories; "I love you too! I love you too!" How could I have not realized, before this moment, that every minute, every second of my life, somebody has loved me! From my birth, I have been loved. Though I didn't realize it with this magnitude before, I have it now! I understand!

Joy and love and peace exploded in my heart!

The love that has been given to me all my life is now realized in one huge accumulation of emotion. The love each person has given me is like individual gifts deposited in my heart, now coming to maturity and fullness as one big expression of love. It is absolutely overwhelming! Reliving and experiencing these wonderful emotions is joyous beyond compare!

I take a few more steps, and while walking, I feel good in my body. This feeling is like being on earth, outside on a hot, muggy day when out of nowhere, a cool breeze blows across you, so you stop what you're doing and enjoy the refreshing feeling. Well, all I feel here is that refreshing feeling and it doesn't stop! I ask myself if I think I can get used to this all of the time, and the answer is a resounding *yes!*

By now I am almost skipping across the water, when to my utter amazement it gets better! With all these feelings of joy and love comes something else. A wave of anointing from the Holy Spirit comes over me like a tidal wave, covering me with the peace of God! In the midst of these incredibly wonderful emotions comes peace, perfect peace. How can I be exploding with joy, permeated with love, and covered with peace, all at the same time? I can't explain it, but it's true. I have all of this at once, and with a spring in my step too!

So many times in my life I have heard, in sermons and songs, about one blessed day when we go to meet the Lord and cross the River Jordan. On the other side of the River Jordan we'll get our reward and be in heaven with Jesus. Well, if this is it, and I believe it must be, it is not the Jordan River—it's the *Joydan River*! Hallelujah! I'm crossing the River Joydan! The river of joy!

Almost completely across now, I see heaven's landscape more clearly. There is a man walking on the shore, coming from my right and stopping in front of me where I'll come ashore. He looks kind of funny, almost casual in appearance and dress. I have never seen a robe that looks casual before, but his does.

As I depart the river, I notice my feet are slightly in the water up to my ankles. His robe is rolled up at the bottom slightly above his ankles as he is standing in the water also. He has a golden sash high around his waist, with tassels hanging down from it at his side. His sleeves are rolled up to his elbows and his hands are on his hips.

We size each other up and he says, "Well, you made it! Welcome!" I say, "Thank you!"

I reach out to shake his hand, which he takes and pulls me close and hugs me. He has a neatly trimmed beard and long curly black hair that flows down to his shoulders. His smile is infectious, causing me to smile back uncontrollably. I know this is a great man. He asked me if I enjoyed my walk across the Joydan. I stumble back a couple of steps into the water and asked, "What did you call that river?"

He said, "Joydan." I laugh out loud and tell him that's what I thought it should be called.

He says, "I know. I know."

I began to tell him about all the feelings and emotions I felt while walking across, and my amazement that I could even walk across. When he could get a word in he said, "I know. I know."

I realize I am rambling on like a boy telling his dad about the great ballgame he had, and about saving the day with a great play. I slow down and gather myself. He is amused at my excitement and is obviously pleased with my arrival and reaction. He tells me how amazed he was the first time he walked on water; and still being charged up from my experience, I politely pretend to listen.

We walk the shore a bit and I ask him what we are doing. I wonder what will happen next. He stops walking and we stand side by side facing the river. With his left arm around my shoulder, he says that if this were my final crossing, others would have been here to greet me, along with him. Family and friends would have greeted me with hugs and love. We would reacquaint ourselves, and they would introduce me to family I have never met. After a time of greeting and fellowship, they would lead me to our heavenly home and go on from there.

But this was not that great final crossing for me, and although I received a taste of it, the best is yet to come. I say, "Wow! That was a taste?" I can't imagine what the real thing will be like. I can't wait!

He chuckles and says, "Yes you can. When the time comes, you'll be ready."

There is something about him that seems so familiar yet I know we have never met. Maybe I just know of him. My curiosity gets the best of me, so as we begin to walk again I ask him, "Who are you? Have I heard of you before? You seem so familiar."

He looks over at me, and with a big smile and a gleam in his eye, he says, "Just call me the Beachcomber."

I think to myself, *The Beachcomber?* We continue to walk along the shore at the water's edge.

You guide me with your counsel, and afterward you will take me into glory.[4]

Chapter 11

The Beachcomber

The beachcomber and I walk slowly along the shore upstream. He tells me, "You are going to witness something very private and personal. No matter what, you may not intrude upon or even speak to those you are about to see. You may, however, speak to me and ask me anything you wish. Do you understand?"

"Yes." I reply. I become very apprehensive about what I am about to see. I know it must be good, but why must I not intrude or speak? I suppose I'll find out soon enough.

The Homecoming

We come to an area that is breathtakingly beautiful. There are steep cliffs on our right and the river is on our left. The scene looks surreal. We walk between the river and the cliffs, and then come out into a clearing, just past the cliffs. From the clearing I see people coming.

They are walking from the right, at a brisk pace, toward the shore. They are laughing and talking to one another all at the same time! What a happy group they are! The beachcomber and I stop about forty yards from their path and observe the scene. About that time, one lady shouts out, "There she is! I see her! Hurry everyone!" And with that, they all run the remaining thirty or more yards to the water's edge.

In the distance I can see the figure of a person walking across the river. I strain my eyes to see. Eventually, the person they are waiting for gets close enough for me to see. Behind her are two angels. I don't think she even knows that they are there because they are behind her and seem to be floating just slightly above the water, not walking on it. I wonder if there were two angels behind me when I crossed. Maybe they are behind me now. I quickly whirl around to catch them, and to my surprise, I see nothing.

"What are you doing?" the beachcomber asks.

Feeling silly I replied, "Nothing, nothing at all."

He says, "Watch."

I look back at the person coming and fall to my knees. I know this lady. She is an old friend who recently passed away. My heart bursts with joy, and my mind swims in shock as I am privileged to see my friend's homecoming! She looks incredible! I have never seen her look so beautiful. Her face glows with the glory of God, and the smile bursting across her face tells me that she must have experienced the joy I got a taste of when I crossed. She wears a robe of white with a gold sash around her waist.

There is a glow of light around her, and as I look into her face, I notice that her hair is illuminated with light. The glory of God is all over her!

She stops short, about fifteen yards from the shore, and her jaw drops. With her mouth wide open I hear her utter, "Oh." Then louder she says, "Oh!" Then again and again she says, "Oh, oh, oh" louder as she begins to run toward the group that is waiting for her.

I look back at the group and a man steps forward out of the crowd. I recognized him! He is her uncle who passed on just a couple of years before. I knew him also. He runs to the river with his arms open wide for her and the last few feet between them she literally jumps into his arms.

He holds her up off the ground and they spin around and around. They are screaming with joy! They say that they love each other over and over again, and then praise the Lord at the top of their lungs. Now I know why the beachcomber told me not to intrude or even speak, as I have to use all my self-control to not run over to them and join in on their rejoicing. I will just have to rejoice over here on my own. I throw my arms around the beachcomber and lift him up off the ground and yell, "I know them! I know her!"

As I begin to tell him my relationship to her and her family, He laughs and says, "I know, Son, I know!" Laughing he says, "Set me down, please. Ha! Ha! Set me down."

Immediately I put him down and smooth out his robe on his shoulders. He sort of stretches his arms to readjust his clothing, and then he says again, "Watch!"

Looking back at the reunion, I see family and friends, one after another, embrace and welcome the dear sister who has just arrived. She is so happy!

I hear her say to another lady, "This is it? I made it?"

Then the older lady replies, "Yes, honey, this is it. You really made it. You really did." With that, they embrace again. She puts one arm around her uncle and they begin to walk home. Others start to gather around them and follow, but as they do, just before they obscure my view of her, she turns her head in my direction.

I think to myself, *Can she see me?*

I get my answer as she mouths the words, "Bye. See you later."

I can't hear for all the noise her family is making, but I saw her mouth the words and I know she saw me.

I know she is happy. She turns and walks away, surrounded by loved ones, heading for their heavenly home where I know the Lord waits. Another saint has come home. Hallelujah! What an honor to witness this. Peace, joy, and safety are just a few of the emotions we experience as we…"cross over." I think it is time for me to go, but the beachcomber says to me, "Come, there are others we must look for."

He begins to walk, and surprised that I could continue, I run to catch up to him. The beachcomber bends over and picks up a long stick. It's twisted at the top and slightly curved. It is about four inches thick from the middle up, and tapered down to about two inches at the bottom tip. When I catch up to him, he is holding it in his right hand and dragging it behind him. I think it is a little strange. What purpose does this serve?

Every so often he surveys the horizon across the river. He is looking for something, or someone. He stops, and with his left hand held over his eyes like a visor, he says, "There! Look!"

I look but see nothing. He tells me to look again. I sit down beside him, as he stands, and strain to see, but still I see nothing.

Then I hear music. It sounds sweet, like children's music. He steps toward the water and I finally see what he sees…a little girl. She is small and is being led by angels. These angels look like children also. They aren't, but their size and demeanor make them look young. An angel is on each side of her holding a hand. She looks so happy!

They stop right in front of the beachcomber. She looks up into his smiling face and asks, "Are you the great shepherd?" Now, it makes sense to me why he has that stick. He is holding it like a shepherd's staff and so he does look like a shepherd. Somehow this is comforting to her.

He tells her, "No, dear, but I know Him."

She points to me and asks if I am the great shepherd. We both say no as I shake my head.

I hear someone behind me and as He speaks, I recognize His voice. Jesus touches me on my shoulder as He passes, and looking down at the little girl He says, "I am the Shepherd, dear one. Come to Me."

Her eyes got as big as silver dollars and her mouth gaped open as she gasped. Then, with the biggest smile you could imagine, she ran past the beachcomber straight into the arms of Jesus. With her arms around His neck and His arms around her waist, He raises her up and they "squeeze the stuffing" out of each other!

He set her down and she walks over to the beachcomber and hugs him. She smiles at me as the Lord scoops her up and holds her with His right arm. With her left arm around His neck, they walk away cheek to cheek.

I ask the beachcomber why no family was here to greet her.

He says, "She came a little unexpected. The Lord is taking her to her fathers." She looks about six years of age. I can only imagine why she came unexpectedly.

I react fast and catch the staff with both hands as he suddenly tosses it to me. He says, "Try this," then turns around and walks up the beach. Funny thing, the length of the stick and the place my hand grips it, fits me like a glove. It is as if it was made for me.

We walk for quite a while and everything in sight is so beautiful! The river is on the left, and on the right, we pass cliffs, meadows, grasslands, rocky hills, sand dunes, and about every type of terrain imaginable.

The Boy

The beachcomber bends over and picks up a short stick. As we walk, he flips it up in the air and catches it. He does it over and over again. Sometimes he flips it up, then turns around and catches it behind his back.

When he does that, he laughs out loud and says, "Did you see that, my friend?" Bending over, with my hands on my knees, I just laugh and laugh. He is so funny!

As we sit I ask, "Are you a juggler?"

He says, "You mean, like robbing Peter to pay Paul?" My eyes got big and so did his, and then we both broke out into hysterical laughter. I laugh so hard I have to hold my sides, and so does he. I am so blessed, seeing saints come home! I am so happy! This is great!

Suddenly, the beachcomber jumps to his feet. He stands and surveys the river. I have come to know what this means. Someone is coming. Just then, I hear barking coming from behind us. I reel around just in time to see the biggest, shaggiest dog I have ever seen run and jump up on me.

I stumble backward and pat him as he has his two front paws on my chest. He gets down and almost hops over to the beachcomber and stands at his heel. The beachcomber pats him on the head as they both look out across the river.

I see him!

I think I see him first because when I say it, the beachcomber says, "Yes, you're right. There he is."

A young boy is coming. He looks to be about eleven or twelve years of age. He is smiling and looking around. The expression on his face changes from happiness to one of extreme excitement when he sees us. Or should I say when he sees the dog. The dog bolts from the beachcomber and heads straight for the boy as he steps ashore.

He bends down and the dog knocks him on his back and stands over him, licking his face with a big, wet tongue. The boy laughs and keeps saying, "Stop, stop." Between laughter, he rubs the dog's sides with his hands. Two long lost friends are reunited at this moment, and it is beautiful! Getting up, the boy brushes himself off and looks toward us. The beachcomber tosses the boy the short stick he holds in his left hand.

With a big grin, the boy says, "Thanks, Mister!" The boy then does the only thing he can do. He throws the stick and says, "Fetch!"

The dog obediently chases after the stick and brings it back. While they are doing this over and over again, I notice a group of people coming. They approach the boy and greet him with hugs and kisses. Then they leave together for home. Wow! What a beautiful sight! Praise God!

We spend our time on the beach, greeting saints as they cross over. There are people of all ages and nationalities, in all shapes and sizes. Most of them cross alone, but some come with groups. All are happy after crossing the Joydan River. However, even after seeing everything I have seen, nothing prepares me for what is coming next…nothing.

The Martyrs

I hear tones of music. It sounds like three different church bells that ring three different notes. Ding-dong. Ding-dong. Note; lower note, note, and even lower note. The musical tones seem to come from above and around us. Then I hear voices singing with the music sounds. Soft and ever so slight, they are high-pitched, yet very clear.

They sing, "Jesus loves me. Jesus loves me." Ding-dong. Ding-dong. Ding-dong. Ding-dong. "Jesus loves me. Jesus loves me."

In the distance across the river we see them approach.

Fellowship in the Spirit

In front and center is an angel. She has a motherly face that shines, no, radiates the love and the glory of God. She is leading little babies wearing white robes.

They are singing, "Jesus loves me. Jesus loves me," over and over again.

They look happy. There are thousands of them, and their number stretches across the river as far back as the eye can see. Standing on the shore facing them, the beachcomber lifts his arms straight out from his side and says, "Welcome home, children! Welcome home!"

They continue singing, "Jesus loves me. Jesus loves me," as they come ashore.

They pass him like a wave coming ashore, and he stands steady, not moving, like a lone post in a rising tide. I stand back about fifty yards and watch them pass. They are wearing tiny white robes and look like premature newborns, but they walk and walk, and sing and sing. The angel leading them has the most beautiful motherly face imaginable!

She leads them past us and up a hill toward the temple of God. As they approach the temple, they become quiet. The singing and music stops. A holy hush comes over them as they march up the hill and into the temple.

The cry of the martyrs in the sixth chapter of the book of Revelation comes to mind. *"How long, O Lord, holy and true, doest thou not judge and avenge our blood on them that dwell on the earth? And white robes were given to every one of them; and it was said unto them, that they should rest yet for a little season, until their fellow servants also and their brethren, that should be killed as they were, should be fulfilled."*

The beachcomber and I stand together and watch their backs as they leave.

I say to him, "They aren't expected today are they?"

"No," he says.

I fall to my knees and weep. Looking up at him, I ask, "All of these were killed in one day?"

"Yes," he says.

I shake my head in disbelief.

He continues, "It's the same every day. Some days there are more than others, but I always find them crossing… always."

"What will happen to them?" I ask.

He says, "They are going to be honored as martyrs and then eventually united with their families here whom they have never met. Remember the joy your memories gave you as you crossed the Joydan?"

"Yes," I reply.

Well, sad to say, the only joy they have to remember is the love they feel from the angel who met them and brought them here. She wiped the tears from their eyes and told them about Jesus, and how He loves them. The thought that He loves them gives them the only joy they have ever experienced. They rejoice on that alone. Praise God that's plenty, right?" he says.

As I watch the last of the little ones fade into the distance, I reply, "Yes. That's enough."

He puts his arm around my shoulder and leads me on, along the shore of the River Joydan.

Precious in the sight of the LORD is the death of his saints.[1]

The Waterfall

The river began to narrow as we continue to walk upstream. We come upon a place that looks so pleasing and inviting. On the left is the river, and on the right is a beautiful meadow surrounded by forest. The oval shaped meadow is about fifty yards long and thirty yards wide. It has beautiful grass about four inches high and is bordered by multicolored flowers.

This is a perfect place for a picnic by the river. Up about twenty yards is a waterfall. It's about twelve feet high and water pours peacefully over its side. I remember now that I've been here before, however I came in from the forest to our right and through the meadow.

I run ahead of the beachcomber, straight to the waterfall. Stepping carefully on a big rock on the water's edge, I slip in behind the waterfall. I stand there and lean my back against the wall and rest. The air is so pure and fresh, I just have to take some deep breaths and get my full enjoyment. I reach my hands into the waterfall and it parts like a curtain of velvet water. I play with it for a while, using my hands to open the curtain of water and peer through to the other side.

Later, I hear the beachcomber call for me. Calling out to him from behind the water, I look up and there he sits. He is sitting on the edge of the waterfall with his legs dangling over the side, in the water. I have done this before and remember how great it feels. Climbing up and walking over to sit down beside him, I have no fear of falling. After all, this is heaven! I sit beside him with my legs also dangling over the side like his, and lean back on my hands, which are in the water, pressing against the bottom.

The water is only waist deep as we sit in the flow. Under my hands I feel something round and smooth so I pick it up to see.

"Oh yeah," I say, "jewels." When I was here before I discovered that the bottom is covered with perfect, priceless, pristine jewels of every kind. What I hold in my hand is an emerald. Now I'm no expert on fine jewelry, but this thing is more magnificent than any emerald on earth I've ever heard about. Holding it up to the sky between my thumb and forefinger, I think about my treasure in heaven, and how…this isn't it.

I ask the beachcomber, "May I?"

He graciously replies, "But of course."

Without any hesitation, I rear back and throw that emerald! We roar with laughter as it skips across the surface of the Joydan River, and then sinks to the bottom. I reach back and pick up another one and examine it to make sure it is of the same quality as the one I have just pitched. As I hold it up, I hear the beachcomber say, "May I?"

With my eyebrows raised in surprise, I reply, "But of course!"

He takes it, rears back and throws it about two feet farther than mine. We laugh hilariously! When we gather ourselves, we both reach back behind us and pull three or four jewel stones to throw, when I hear a slight splash to my right.

Quickly I turn, and sitting in the water beside me on my right, was the Master, Lord Jesus Himself. I almost fall over the waterfall in surprise, but they each grabbed an arm and steady me.

With His right hand extended to us, palm up, He looks at us and says, "May I?"

The beachcomber and I look at each other, then back at Him, and say in unison, "But of course!" We all three laugh out loud. Once we settle down, we both hand Him all of our stones.

He studies them carefully and then selects the best one. He leans over to me and says, "Wish me well!"

I say, "Yes, Lord. Praise you, Lord!"

Softly and deliberately shaking His head back and forth,

He chuckles and says, "That's good. Thank you!" He rears back and lets it fly!

I think to myself, *That jewel is going out of this realm and into the next.*

Knowing my thoughts, the Lord says, "Nah, it wasn't that great!"

I think to myself, *Jesus said, "nah"?*

He looks over at me and says, "Yep!"

I lose it! I mean this is too much! The three of us laugh and laugh! The jewel, by the way, hit the water where ours sank, and skipped on down the river out of sight!

After a time of playing and fellowship, Lord Jesus, the beachcomber, and I get up and walk down to the meadow. We all lay on our backs with our feet flat on the ground and our knees sticking up. The beachcomber is on my left and Lord Jesus is on my right. We talk about anything and everything. Then there are times when not a word is spoken. We listen to the peaceful sound of the waterfall as the river flows by.

The Lord begins to talk about His church, and the order of things. He explains how He originally set up the organization of the church, and then asks, "Isn't that right?"

The beachcomber replies, "Yes, Lord. It is so."

Sometimes in reply to Jesus, the beachcomber slaps me on my left knee and says "Yep!"

They're really having fun with that "yep" word. I can see from the perspective of the Lord's pure heart what He desires in a church, and His love, His unconditional love for His church.

I tell Him, "Lord, I only hope I can be part of a great church like that. Make us, make me, like that." Jesus turns and smiles at me.

The Beachcomber

The beachcomber slaps my knee again and says, "Friend, you are already in His church. You are in His presence! That's church! This is it! This is what He left us and charged us to share and pass down to the next generation! This is it. Don't you understand how He desires all of His children to share in moments like these? Many in the early church did so, but it's been a long time, too long, since He has had a body to abandon their selves completely, fully, and in unity to Him. It's been so long, He wants it back."

"Yes I do," says the Lord. "Son," Jesus says, "everyone is welcome here. Everyone! To come to the Father they must come through Me. You and others have come through Me. Anyone who will, they can come through Me. Son, point them to Me. There is enough religion. I appreciate their efforts, but mostly they are missing one small detail…Me! True religion is to love Me, desire Me, and seek Me…for Me. I have sought you and them. Point them to Me."

I rise up to my knees and face Him, and then I fall on my face, prone on the ground. He sits up and gently strokes the hair on the back of my head like a parent would.

"Believe me," He says, "church is not a building. Do you see any building here, where we are?"

"No, Lord," I reply.

"Do you see a written creed or any denominational church organization?"

"No, Lord," I reply.

He leans over and puts His lips close to my ear and quietly says, "Do you see a sign with a pastor's name on it?"

Chuckling to myself I say, "I get it, Lord. I get it."

With a friendly slap on the back He says, "Get up now!"

"OK, Lord," I reply.

Fellowship in the Spirit

As I sit up facing them, He turns to the beachcomber and says, "Peter, tell him!"

I know my jaw hit my chest as I looked at the beachcomber. He looks over at the Lord with an expression that says, "Now why did You do that?"

Jesus laughs and says, "Come on now, it's OK! We're all friends here. You know, brothers…family."

Peter looks back at me, as if to say, "Sorry I didn't tell you earlier."

I take a deep breath and cry. The tears just stream down my face as I realize the full ramification of what just happened. This is Peter! *On this rock I will build my church!* Saint Peter meeting us at the pearly gate! All the references to Peter come back to me. He searches the River Joydan's shores to prepare and greet the saints as they cross over. He doesn't wait until they get to the gates. What a servant our beachcomber is. What love he has for the saints and for the Master he serves!

Overwhelmed as I am, I beg him to tell me. "What was it like?" I asked. "Tell me about that great day of Pentecost and the upper room. Tell me about your days with Jesus when He walked and lived among you and the people! I want to hear it all!"

Lord Jesus stands and walks between where we are sitting crossed legged, facing each other. He puts a hand on each of our heads and says, "I love you. I love you both. Enjoy each other. Share and be…be My church."

I thought to myself that two of us are together in His name and He is in the midst of us. As He walks away, I still feel like He is here. He *is* still here. Turning to Peter, I reach out my hands and clasp both of his hands. I pull him toward me and plead with him, "Tell me. Now, tell me!"

He does, and it is wonderful! Praise God what a

testimony! I stay with him for what seems like days, and then it is time for me to continue on. I have really made a friend, mentor, and father. I cannot believe how truly blessed I am. This Lord, this friend, this fellowship in the Spirit! This church!

> *For where two or three come together in my name, there am I with them.*[2]

Chapter 12

Our Family Home

There are so many things I love about heaven and walking in the Spirit. I love to serve the Lord in the temple, to intercede with Him at the altar of incense. I love spending time with Father, Lord Jesus, and the Holy Spirit together and individually. What a privilege! I love just sitting outside the temple on the steps watching the activities of heaven. But there's also a place that beckons me, a place that we're all drawn to eventually. That place is our family home.

As I walk alongside the river of life outside the city, going away from the city, I see many houses. They are all riverfront property so to speak, the riverfront of life property. As I walk on the right side of the river on a path, there is such peace and purity. This is a place never soiled, much less spoiled. On my left between the path and the river are trees with various fruit on each one. I enjoy a piece while I sit on the riverbank with my feet in the water. Leaning back on my hands, I hold my head back and look up, seeing a beautiful bird sitting on a limb, singing a song for my enjoyment.

Upward, through the limbs, I can see the sky. Oh, how beautiful it is! Everything here is beautiful, but it's time to walk on. I pass a family home. People are inside and some are outside. It's a large house and contains many people. I hear the laughter and joy of fellowship as I pass. I can't help but smile as I think of how happy they are to be there, to be together.

There are turns in the river of life, and around every bend is a breathtaking scene of the nature of heaven. Dotting either side of the river throughout this heavenly nature are family homes. Before I walked here in the spirit, I thought we were all going to have our own private mansion. And in a sense we do, but it's not one mansion per person. If that were the case, there would be many empty mansions in heaven. Nobody here wants to live alone. They are too busy having fellowship.

Although there are dwelling places such as in Father's house where you can be alone, and places like this arbor I'm approaching where you can have solitude, I've never seen a private house for a single person. No, I've seen something much more wonderful!

I am entering a small arbor beside the river of life behind my family home. The layout is like this. There's the river, beside which are fruit trees. Next is this arbor in which I am now sitting. Beside the arbor is the path, which runs parallel along the entire length of the river. From that path, a walkway leads to my family home.

I can see it as I sit here. There is a beautiful garden between here and the actual building. This is a garden of low hedges and flowers, somewhat like an elegant English garden. On either side of the house and garden is the forest of God. On this magnificent house, which faces the river and myself, is a large porch with round columns and steps that appear to be made of marble.

There isn't a door, only a doorway. This is my house but not mine alone. All of my family, and ancestors, dwell here. It's a place where we all belong. So many people on earth are estranged from family, separated in some way, or maybe even orphaned. It is not good for people to be alone forever. Here, we all have the family we have dreamed of on earth. Here, family is everything, and our heavenly Father is the head.

I suppose if people wanted, really wanted their own private house, Father would give it to them. But heaven is a place to share and I can't imagine living alone.

I sit and look at our family home and I know that inside are my mother, father, grandparents, great grandparents, and so forth. What do they think of all this? What do they think of me? Do they know I'm here? Somehow I think they do, but that doesn't matter. I know I'm not allowed to fully partake of heaven just yet. This is only a glimpse. But it's good to hear their laughter, see their shadows move across the windows and door way. I'm content to sit here and watch, knowing that they are there and always will be.

> *And he shewed me a pure river of water of life, clear as crystal, proceeding out of the throne of God and of the Lamb. In the midst of the street of it, and on either side of the river, was there the tree of life, which bare twelve manner of fruits, and yielded her fruit every month: and the leaves of the tree were for the healing of the nations.*[1]

Chapter 13

God Is Light

When we meet God, the Three, in Their unity as One, we meet Yahweh. This is such a Holy state of Their being that the name Yahweh wasn't even spoken by the children of Israel. Though we are born again and in Them and are allowed to speak Their name, we must still be reverent, respectful, and in total awe of the name, and referring to Them in that state.

Apostle John wrote, *"God is light; in him there is no darkness at all. If we claim to have fellowship with him yet walk in the darkness, we lie and do not live by the truth. But if we walk in the light, as he is in the light, we have fellowship with one another, and the blood of Jesus, his Son, purifies us from all sin."*[1]

There is a realm of God, a realm of light, where we can go in Him. As I shared before, when we join them at the ark in heaven we experience the light. And there are times when we see the Lord Jesus or Father in Their glory where we glimpse the light, but there is a realm of light itself where we exist in Them; and as John said, we walk with them there.

It is written in the book of Job, *"What is the way to the abode of light?"*[2] I am convinced that Job must have caught a glimpse of this light. If we trust in the Lord, He is faithful to share everything with us. He holds nothing back, and the Holy Spirit leads us into all truth. Turn your desires away from the things of the earth and toward the things of heaven and the realm of God in the light.

"Blessed are those who have learned to acclaim you, who walk in the light of your presence, O Lord."[3] Walking in the light with God is His desire for us. Paul wrote to the Colossians, *"Giving thanks to the Father, who has qualified you to share in the inheritance of the saints in the kingdom of light."*[4] And to the Thessalonians, *"You are all sons of the light and sons of the day."*[5]

A City of Light

One evening I heard the Spirit calling me to pray. As I closed my eyes I was immediately caught up in the Spirit. When my spiritual eyes opened, I found myself standing on a ledge, an outcropping of rocks, on a great mountain. Darkness surrounded the scene and yet clouds were visible, which appeared even darker. As I looked to my left, I beheld the Lord Jesus. He was standing, and His robe and hair flowed gently in the wind. He was looking straight ahead with His right hand lifted to touch His beard ever so slightly. He was intently studying something in the distance.

Looking to my right, to my amazement, I saw what He was looking at so intently. It was a city of light! Below and to the east was a glow of light in the darkness, which covered the city like a dome. Looking intently at the city, I tried to discern its features; admittedly I was caught up in the "other worldliness" of it. Wow, what a sight!

My concentration was broken by the touch of the Lord Jesus grasping my left hand. I looked down at my hand in His and He said, "Son, let's go. Are you ready?"

I said, "Yes, Lord. I believe I am." Immediately we began to float away from the mountain and down toward the city of light. I didn't look over, up, or down. All I could focus on was the city. As we approached it, the brightness increased. I asked, "Lord, is this the city of light?"

He replied, "It is a city of light. There are more than one. Let Me show you." About that time my feet touched the ground and we began to walk. Still, He did not let go of my hand, and I was very glad for I could not see clearly. Everything was so bright. It was like looking into the sun, except that it didn't hurt, I just couldn't see.

Well, we walk on and I notice buildings and dwelling places. But there is such a glare on them and brightness coming from them that it is impossible to describe them. Let me describe it in the opposite. You know how it looks on a darkened street at night, very black with even darker shadows encompassing different nooks and corners? Well it's the same with the light. Everything is so bright and then there are splashes of even brighter light that encompass different nooks and corners.

Had the Lord Jesus not had a firm grip on my hand, I would have surely bumped into things. After a few steps, I was aware of beings approaching us. These beings were even brighter than anything I had seen yet. They spoke a language all their own. I didn't understand it at first, but what I did understand was the love and emotion lavished on Jesus on a level unparalleled by any human attempt of the same. The Lord allowed me to feel the emotion of the love and adoration being directed at Him. It was so precious, intimate, and sacred. These beings continued to gather around and worship Jesus. It seemed so personal that I felt a little uncomfortable being there. This adoration should have been private.

More and more gathered, and not just around us. I could make out beings of light above us. I could not make out their features for the light in and around them all was far too bright. The Lord had me cover my eyes and peep through my fingers a glimpse. When I did, the brightness was eased somewhat and I could see that these beings weren't human.

"They are angels," Jesus said, "and this city of light is their abode." They are creatures of light in a city of light. This is where they live when they are not on assignment for Me or Father."

I was blown away! It is a city of light inhabited by angels. "What do they do here Lord?" I asked.

"They do the things that angels do," He said, with a twinkle in His eyes. I had to admit, He did catch me off guard with His humor. He's so cool.

"What are the things that angels do Lord?" I asked.

"Well," He said, "They sing and play musical instruments. They practice and develop new music to present to Us, Father, Holy Spirit, and Me. They dance and fight. They practice spiritual warfare. They study the Godhead and try to emulate every aspect of Our beings. They strive to be like Us so that they might please Us. And they rest, play, and live a life of peace in the glory of their Lord."

I strained to look at them, but I could not make out any discernable features. This was frustrating. To be so close, yet it's like looking through a glass brightly. As I squinted to see, the light subsided ever so slightly, and what I beheld, I am at a loss of words to describe.

Whoa! I am startled. Father is approaching. The way He looks is breathtaking and surreal. I am at a loss of words to describe the details of His appearance other than to say as it is written in the Bible, *"God is light; in him there is no darkness at all."*[6]

I fell prostrate before Him and worshipped, as did all the beings of light. As they all fell to the ground, it was like a fog of light covered the ground, and I was part of it. I could not make out where one being ended and the other began. They seemed to be intermingled as one, yet they were separate.

There was literally a ground swell of praise that roared from the ground to our Father. Then they began to swirl in a circle around us, Father, Lord Jesus, and me. The fog of light moved faster and faster round and round us, and then they were gone. We were left alone, just the three of us.

The Lord Jesus, who had never let go of my hand, pulled me up from the ground to stand with them. As I beheld the face of Father, I could see Him in the glory of His light as never before. He is light! He smiled and reached forward for me. For the first time since being here, the Lord Jesus let go of my hand just as Father embraced me.

He held me in His arms longer than I expected and said, "Feel Me, Son? Feel the part of Me that you are?"

"Yes Father," I replied. "I feel like I have sunk into You and am an actual part of You."

"You have it!" Father proclaimed. "Jesus, he has it!"

"Yes Father, I agree," Lord Jesus said. "Son," Father said, "in this realm of light, we are free to move among, in, and through one another as one. This is part of My glory. You are in Me as I am in you, and we are in Them as They are in us, as a part of Our all in all. It is so easy to fellowship one with another here, isn't it?"

"Yes, Father, it truly is." I replied. "Will I ever leave here?" I asked. "It feels permanent and everlasting."

"Yes, Son, you are about to go back. I don't want you to just have head knowledge to share about My realms of light. I wanted you to have a real feeling for the place. Tell My children about the glory that is theirs, even as it is yours and Mine today."

"Tell My children about the glory that is theirs..."

Immediately I felt myself drifting, no, floating back to the ledge on the side of the mountain where this all began. Father waved goodbye to us as Jesus held a firm grip on my hand. My Father, whom I love so much, faded into the distance. Upon returning to the rock ledge, I found myself looking at that city of light once again. Jesus, as before, was standing just a few feet to my left. He smiled and nodded His head, just before I came back to myself here on earth.

Because of the beauty and magnificence of this place, I can see why Father spends time there. To think that He would actually come down to heaven from the realm of light so that He might fellowship with us in the Spirit is incredible! Fellowship in the Spirit leads ultimately to fellowship in the light. It was true for the apostles and the early church, and it is just as true for us today.

The Lord encourages us to enjoy the growth, so seek Him in His realm of light. Ask the Holy Spirit to enable your spirit to grow. When we do our part by feeding our spirit with daily Bible reading, study, and with prayer in the Spirit, He'll do His part by bringing us into His realm of light. It is a glorious process! God never ceases to amaze me. Just when I think He has given me the ultimate experience, He tops it with another. He'll do the same for you.

Chapter 14

Angels

Other than the Lord Himself, perhaps no other religious subject has been written about as much as the subject of angels. Even the secular world holds a fascination with the existence of angels. We have seen how even the entertainment industry has portrayed the existence of angels, mostly in error, and contrary to the Word of God.

As you fellowship in the Spirit with the Lord, or are led of the Spirit into the realms of heaven in prayer, it is inevitable that you will encounter angels. So much has been written about angels that entire sections of bookstores display book after book on the subject. Be that as it may, some books are good, but many have errors, so it is important that we as children of God know the truth about angels. Father wants us to know about the family servants.

There are pitfalls to be avoided in associating with them, because the enemy has multitudes of fallen angels to use against believers. I have experienced the true angels of God—and the tricky, sneaky angels of light that work for the devil. The angels of the Lord represent the highest standard of honor, courage, strength, and righteousness in the realm of the Spirit. They represent the Lord, and as such should be held in high esteem and respect.

We'll explore what the Word of God teaches, and I'll also share my own experiences with angelic encounters.

Angels Attend God's Throne

The prophet Isaiah wrote, *"In the year that king Uzziah died I saw also the Lord sitting upon a throne, high and lifted up, and his train filled the temple. Above it stood the seraphims: each one had six wings; with twain he covered his face, and with twain he covered his feet, and with twain he did fly. And one cried unto another, and said, Holy, holy, holy, is the Lord of hosts: the whole earth is full of his glory."*[1]

Apostle John wrote, *"All the angels were standing around the throne and around the elders and the four living creatures. They fell down on their faces before the throne and worshiped God."*[2] John and Isaiah were witnesses to the activity around God's throne in heaven. I also have been privileged to see activity around the throne of grace in heaven. One day while praying in the Spirit, I saw ministering angels walking into the throne room in heaven, with open palms, facing forward, kneeling down before the throne of God.

Father was saying something to them and blessing them. When Father was finished, the angels left heaven and came to earth. There were so many ministering angels that I couldn't count them all. From what I gathered, they were coming to earth to help in soul-winning, priming people to come to the Lord. *"There is rejoicing in the presence of the angels of God over one sinner who repents."*[3] How valuable we must be if a multitude of angels rejoice when just one soul is saved!

Until now, I didn't understand why. They rejoice because they have a hand in every soul that is won. Father sends them to minister to sinners. And when a soul comes to God through Christ, drawn by the Holy Spirit, the ministering angels have succeeded in their part of the mission, so they rejoice! They share in the joy of the Lord!

Angels were everywhere, above and below, over and around the throne in vast innumerable ranks. Not only do the angels serve God, they worship Him continually. In their worship is an element of studying Him. They sometimes focus their worship on the different attributes of God.

Once an attribute of God is studied, they model it in their own being. How much more should we, His children, study God's attributes and model ourselves after our Father, Lord Jesus, and the Holy Spirit and Their ways.

There are times when the curtain between heaven and earth is pulled back and we experience our earthly worship joined with the angel's heavenly worship. One such experience happened at one of our prayer meetings.

On this particular evening, there were about thirteen of us gathered, taking communion when the Holy Spirit fell upon us in a mighty way. We were all praising God and worshipping in the Spirit, and His presence was with us. We sang in the Spirit, prayed in the Spirit, and shouted in the Spirit. It produced a most unusual sound, a cacophony of the sounds of God's people worshipping Him all at once.

In the Spirit, I could see Jesus standing in the middle of our group with us around Him in a circle in heaven, as we were on earth. As we worshipped and praised Him, He had the biggest and most beautiful smile on His face. He looked around at each one of us, one by one as we praised Him. I noticed that above Him and our group, forming a circular canopy, were angels. They observed our worship of Lord Jesus with wonder and marvel.

As I looked up into their faces, they seemed astonished at the worship, communion, and our fellowship. Oh what a beautiful sight! What a beautiful experience!

Many times angels are seen flying in formation or massed together in groups. Once, when Jesus was bringing me back to heaven from the realm of light, I saw a magnificent array of angels. Jesus and I were in the air above heaven, and below us was a canopy of angels. It was like flying in an airplane and looking down at the clouds except that these were angels. They were flying wing tip to wing tip and filled the sky below us. Jesus and I descended through the angels like a plane descends through clouds. What a way to fly!

Angels perform music and sing in heaven in and out of the throne room. Once while praying in the Spirit, I found myself in a beautiful and peaceful setting. Angels passed by carrying musical instruments. One of them stopped, turned around, and held out his instrument so that I could see. It was a stringed instrument smaller than a guitar, larger than a violin, yet wider than a guitar. It was unlike any stringed musical instrument I had ever seen, but it made beautiful music.

I settled in as the angels played and sang. They sang notes in a range higher than could be heard with the human ear on earth. But, here in heaven, it's naturally heard. It was so beautiful and unusual, sung in a language that I didn't understand.

Angels attend to the saints in heaven. The Holy Spirit showed me that great banquet to come, the marriage supper of the Lamb. The banquet table sits on the crystal sea, a table as long as the eye can see, with a rainbow above. The place settings were prepared and the chairs were pulled up to the table. Behind each chair stood an angel, as far down the table as could be seen. They are ministering angels, prepared to serve and wait upon the occupants of those chairs.

One day soon, we the believers, the children of the Most High, will watch, as the angel assigned to our chair will carefully pull it out so that we might sit at the Master's table.

God's Messengers to Mankind

> *But the angel said to them, "Do not be afraid. I bring you good news of great joy that will be for all the people. Today in the town of David a Savior has been born to you; he is Christ the Lord."*[i]

Many Scriptures in the Bible tell of God's messengers delivering His messages to His people and others. They usually deliver the message verbally, but sometimes their message is delivered with action. I remember just such an occasion that happened at my business, in my warehouse.

At the end of the workday, I heard my warehouse manager worshipping God in the warehouse as he worked. The Holy Spirit was manifesting Himself all over my manager. I was sitting at my desk working when the Holy Spirit came over me as well. Another brother and I stepped into the warehouse to see what was going on, and to our surprise, in the Spirit, we saw balls of fire coming from the back of the warehouse to the front. They continued, then, out of the doorway where we stood.

First it would be a ball of fire, and then it would be a wall of fire. When the fire passed the manager, he would speak in tongues, shout to the Lord, and then shake under the anointing. Then as the fire passed us, we would speak in tongues and shake under the anointing as well. Wave after wave of the Holy Spirit came through that warehouse and us.

When this subsided, we went to the back of the warehouse to investigate where the fire was coming from. As we approached the back, the power of God was so strong that we stumbled and could hardly stand. Then we saw him. A huge angel stood facing us. He would slowly bring his large wings together and when they touched, fire would come out and soar through the warehouse.

The three of us stood, worshipping God, and were filled,

no, smothered by the very presence of the Lord. During this, I received a message from the Lord to build a chapel. Over the next few days we cleared the warehouse and built a chapel to meet and worship the Lord, and fellowship in the Spirit in the very place where the angel stood. The blessings that we received in that chapel could fill a book of its own. God brought the anointing and the instructions to build the chapel through that angel.

Personal Guardians

Jewish tradition and folklore speaks of a personal guardian angel, and Christian tradition also hints at such. Jesus said, *"See that you do not look down on one of these little ones. For I tell you that their angels in heaven always see the face of my Father in heaven."*[5] Whether a specific angel is permanently assigned or whether angels are dispatched as needed, I cannot say. It may be both. Daniel recorded an occasion where the archangel, Michael, came to aid him.

The Lord has done it both ways in my experience. He has shown me an individual angel that protects me, and also I have seen huge forces of angels, too large to count.

Divine Agents

God rules all creation and He uses His angels to carry out His commands. We read in the Bible where God uses His angels to carry out judgment and set things right in the last days: *"The Son of Man will send out his angels, and they will weed out of his kingdom everything that causes sin and all who do evil."*[6]

Hierarchy of Angels

Before the Christian era, Jewish teaching depicted an elaborate system of angels, their ranks and duties. There are various writings to which theologians refer in the study of angels. I hold the Bible as absolute truth and these other writings as the testimonial reason of men.

Protestants generally divide the angels into two categories, angel and archangel. Other terms such as dominions, powers, principalities, and so forth are described as functions of angels.

There are seven archangels mentioned by name in various Christian writings. Michael and Gabriel are mentioned in the book of Daniel in the Bible. Another one is mentioned in the Catholic Bible, and four others are mentioned in the book of Enoch. Opinions differ as to the precise nature of the organization of the angels, so I won't muddy the waters with my opinion.

Suffice it to say that there are seven archangels, and when they're together, they usually accompany God. I have seen them in this role several times in the Spirit. When Father appears, especially in a formal setting, the seven archangels are near. Sometimes they line up in front of Him, and other times they line up behind Him.

There will always be debate among theologians. We must take the Bible as our true source of definite fact. The Holy Spirit will reveal what He wants us to understand as it pertains to our lives. With the life and resurrection of Christ, and the gift of the Holy Spirit, angels no longer stand as the primary source of communication between God and man as they did in the pre-Christian days. Angels still bring messages from God, guard believers, bring firsthand reports to God, and carry out all heavenly duties and business from God to all creation.

Number of Angels

There are so many angels, only God knows exactly how many there are. The apostle John wrote, *"Then I looked and heard the voice of many angels, numbering thousands upon thousands, and ten thousand times ten thousand. They encircled the throne...."*[7] Angels do encircle the throne but are not always stationary. They also fly in formation in a circle around the throne, both above and below. It is a sight beyond nature, a tornado of peace and power.

Evil Angels

"God did not spare angels when they sinned, but sent them to hell, putting them into gloomy dungeons to be held for judgment."[8] We know from the Scriptures that a third of the angels fell at the time of Lucifer's rebellion. They became what we know as demons, and have ranks and authority under Satan's dominion.

Their goal is to rule this earth and serve Satan as they formerly served God. They and their evil are very real. One doesn't have to look very hard before their handiwork becomes evident. Without detailing their endless deeds of destruction here, I must still sound a warning.

Beware of angels of light! I speak with firsthand knowledge. I had an occasion when an angel tried to communicate with me and enter into a regular part of my spiritual life. Frankly, I was deceived and thought he was there to help me. Thankfully, Father allowed the experience in order to teach me how subtle and crafty they can be. Also, Father surrounded me with His angels to protect me and actually render the angel of light powerless.

Paul tells us, *"Satan himself masquerades as an angel of light. It is not surprising, then, if his servants masquerade as servants of righteousness."*[9] We must pray that the Lord will give us spiritual discernment and protection from the enemy's deception. Do not fall into angel worship or intense relationships with spiritual beings. Paul wrote the church a warning:

Do not let anyone who delights in false humility and the worship of angels disqualify you for the prize. Such a person goes into great detail about what he has seen, and his unspiritual mind puffs him up with idle notions.[10]

Make sure your walk in the Spirit is rooted and grounded in the Lord, in the Holy Spirit, and covered by the blood of Jesus. Any other spiritual relationship should be suspect. The Lord doesn't mind if you check the spirits even when you are with Him! It doesn't hurt His ego at all. His Holy Word warns us to check the spirits for a reason. Danger!

The longer you fellowship in the Spirit with the Lord Jesus, Father, and the Holy Spirit, the more clearly you are able to discern Their voice. His sheep knows His voice. We must hold tightly to the truths of the Bible and the safety that it gives. When you run your spiritual experience through the searchlight of God's Word, the truth will come out and your spiritual experience will be edified.

People may witness the same event or experience with a different interpretation, but that doesn't invalidate the experience. The Holy Spirit will give us what we need, individually and corporately, out of a given experience. There is no limit to what the Holy Spirit can do. As scary as possible deception is, we can trust the Holy Spirit to keep us, even through a deception, and bring us to the correct and righteous understanding. We must not let enemy attacks stop our fellowship in the Spirit—just the opposite. When attacked, we need fellowship even more!

Chapter 15

Angelic Encounters

It never fails that as I prepare to teach about angels, and in this case write about them, the Lord will give me a firsthand experience to share. As I prepared to write this chapter, the Holy Spirit gave me a vision concerning an angel, a fresh vision.

Angels in the Spirit

For two days, every time I closed my eyes to pray, I found myself in the Spirit looking at an angel, and the garment he wore. I am about six feet two inches tall, standing toe to toe with this angel, and I look straight into his chest. So, based on that, I would say that he is about eight feet tall. He wears a white garment, which ripples as the wind blows upon us gently from my right.

As wind blows his garment tight against him, I can see the outline of his physique, which appears muscular, strong and powerful. His height, combined with a powerful appearance, makes him quite intimidating. Yet he stands quiet and peaceful, allowing me to stand and stare. My attention turns to his garment's design. A jewel-studded ribbon, about four inches wide, adorned the center of his garment from the top at the neck, down to the waist, and then around each side.

The smallest jewel was larger than any jewel I have seen on earth, and each one has its own unique color and cut. They all glisten with the light and glory of God. The Spirit led me to reach out and touch one of the jewels. Instantly my vision changed places and time. I saw the angel fighting in a fierce battle with fire all around him. He wielded a mighty sword in his right hand, swinging it from left to right, slaughtering everything in its path. Men and horses alike fell under the hand of this warrior angel.

He single handedly destroyed an entire army of mighty men of renown. When the battle was over, not one man, not one horse, was left alive. The angel surveyed the battlefield, and when he was sure his mission was complete, he returned to the Lord. The jewel I touched, that allowed me to see this battle, was given to the angel as a medal, a reward for his bravery and success in this battle. The Holy Spirit had me stand there and touch jewel after jewel, which enabled me to see exploit after exploit in which this angel was involved. Once, the angel dammed up a river to keep a town downstream from being flooded and destroyed.

One rather large jewel was given to him for a battle against an army of demons. When I touched it, immediately I was on a battlefield. Looking around all I saw was scorched earth with wisps of smoke rising up to a darkened angry sky. In the distance, a large cloud of red dust rose from the earth like a specter. I could hear the thunderous sound of a vast horde of demons approaching fast and furious.

This was my perspective as I stood behind the angel and peered around his right side. He stood with a wide stance, his fists planted firmly on his sides. Taking a couple of steps back, I noticed he didn't have wings. He looked to his left and then to his right. Following his glance, to my surprise, there were three angels on either side of him and they were just as imposing as he.

The hordes of demons were almost upon them when all seven angels, simultaneously, stretched forth their right hands. As they did, swords of light appeared, held firmly in their grasp. They stood like a wall of light against the hordes of hell. Together they shouted, "For the glory of God! Hallelujah!"

Just then, the demons slammed against them. It was like watching the explosion of a universe. The demons disintegrated as they touched the wall of light formed by the drawn swords. Demon parts were flying everywhere, but disappeared as they hit the ground. This battle went on and on until there was nothing left but a red cloud of dust. When the dust settled, the angels lowered their right hands, and the swords of light that formed the wall of light disappeared. Finally, the angels relaxed their stance, surveyed the scene for a few moments. Then I was back.

I asked the Holy Spirit about this battle, and what He told me was mind-boggling. He told me that this battle was actually my battle. He had sent these angels to protect me against this onslaught meant for my destruction. He further told me that there are many times in Christians lives that battles are fought in the spirit realm, and in the natural, in which our souls and bodies are hanging in the balance. Many times the Lord sends warrior angels and sometimes He will take an active hand and protect us Himself.

Well, as I continued to look at and touch these medals, jewel after jewel gave me the history of the exploits of this mighty angel of the Lord. I had never heard of these exploits before, and they were fantastic. When I finished, I looked up at his face. How do I describe the beauty I beheld? His face was strong, muscular, and masculine. He had a strong chin, a firm jaw, and high cheekbone. His eyes were large, piercing, and sparkled with the fire and color of a peridot stone. His hair, blowing in the wind, was pure white, with a thick metallic texture. His countenance and bearing exuded pure righteousness. This was a holy angel of the Lord, a magnificent being. I found that all of his jeweled medals testified to his heroism.

Angels in the Flesh

Up until now I have discussed angelic encounters in the spirit, but you should know that angels also take on human appearance and form. Have you ever met an angel in person, in the flesh? *"Do not forget to entertain strangers, for by so doing some people has entertained angels without knowing it."[1]* God's Word says it happens, so how do we know it hasn't happened to us?

People have testified as to having unusual exchanges with strangers that later made them wonder, "Was that an angel?" I had just such an experience. I had been preparing to teach my Bible study class a series on angels. The afternoon before my first class, I made a stop at the local Post Office to check my box. It was a bright and sunny Wednesday afternoon. I pulled into the Post Office parking lot and noticed that there were only two cars parked.

Great, I thought, *no crowd at the Post Office today.* As I walked up to enter, a man who was standing just outside the door spoke to me. He asked if I knew where the nearest FedEx office was located. I thought that was strange because not five feet from where we were standing was a FedEx drop box. I pointed that out to him, but he still wanted to know the location of the FedEx office.

I painstakingly gave him detailed directions how to get there. He reached out to shake my hand, and I figured he was about to thank me. He did, but then he did not let go of my hand. He held my hand in a vise-like grip, and didn't let go.

This fellow was of average build and shorter than me. I thought it strange that on a hot, sunny day he wore a brown long-sleeved jacket, and it was zipped up to his chin. He wore khaki pants and brown leather work shoes. He was a nondescript person, one that nobody would notice under normal circumstances. But his countenance was unusual. His hair was dark, straight, and slicked back. His skin was dark olive.

At first I thought he was Hispanic, but as I stood there in his grip I realized that not only was he not Hispanic, his race was really not apparent. He just looked foreign. I began to feel very uncomfortable because this small man had complete control over me. I couldn't move. He held me firmly in his grip as he smiled and said, "You're a kind man."

"Thank you." I said. Then he began to tell me things about myself, encouraging me. He had no way of knowing anything about me, and yet here we were having an intimate, private conversation. When he was through, he released his grip and I hurriedly said goodbye and went inside the Post Office. I had taken two or three steps inside the door when I stopped, turned around abruptly and stepped back outside the glass door where we had been. He was gone!

I looked around the parking lot and saw only three cars parked there, including mine. There was nobody to be found. I hurriedly looked past the parking lot and down the street in both directions, but neither he nor anybody was there. The street and the parking lot were empty. Even the other cars in the parking lot were empty. He had nowhere to go. Where could he have gotten to in three seconds? Nowhere! He just vanished!

I stood in amazement. The encounter was so strange. His knowledge of me was uncanny, even somewhat prophetic. I wondered. Did God do this? Was this an angel? Later that afternoon, I sought the Lord because I wanted to have confirmation. He told me that yes it had been an angel and that He wanted me to have a positive experience to be able to teach. He wanted me to have firsthand experience, not just book knowledge.

Yes, angels are real! As God's children, we have a right and a privilege to see them. Multitudes of angels are sent by God to protect us and fight our battles. Embrace the reality of these magnificent creatures, as they are God's handiwork. They shall remain loyal to Him and to us. Understand that when your spiritual eyes are opened and you have fellowship in the Spirit with the Lord, angels will be seen. They populate the heavenly realm and accentuate the glory and magnificence of God.

Chapter 16

Spiritual Warfare

When Christians use the phrase "spiritual warfare," it could mean a variety of things. The phrase might be used to describe a very serious illness someone is battling, or someone might use it just to describe a bad day. But whatever the intended meaning, most people don't realize that spiritual warfare is a real situation where the forces of God take on the forces of evil, usually on our behalf. What happens in the spiritual realm is played out in the natural realm. So remember, the battles in which we find ourselves on earth are won or lost in the spiritual realm first. Here are a few examples.

One day while praying in the Spirit, the Lord showed me a multitude of angels in heaven. They were gathered in formation outside God's throne room, in the courtyard surrounding the altar. The angels were standing in rank and file formation by groups, with their swords by their sides. There were many groups in formation before the throne, too many to count. The leaders of the groups approached the altar.

A giant pillar of fire, which was the fire of the Holy Ghost, burned upon the altar and rose from the altar all the way up to the third heaven, that next realm of God. The leaders, the angel commanders, lifted their swords as they reached the altar and carefully touched the tip into the fire. I could see energy flow down their swords and into their bodies. The Holy

Spirit energized their swords and their very bodies, and they all began to shine like the sun!

Once the anointing was complete, the angel commanders returned to the groups they commanded and touched the tip of their swords to the tips of the swords of their angels. Once touched, all the angels' swords, as well as the angels, were energized by the Holy Spirit and shone with the brightness of the sun. The army was ready. Next they marched rank and file into the throne room of God. Once assembled, they dropped to one knee and held their swords pointed to the floor. Leaning over their swords, they bowed before God. Group after group did this until there were multitudes of groups of angels, all bowed before God saying, "Holy, holy, holy."

An archangel stood before the Lord with his trumpet ready to blow. The Lord Jesus also stood before the throne, observing the pageantry of the angel army entering in and honoring Father and Him saying, "Holy, holy, holy."

When their worship was complete, they flew up from the throne room and out of the top. Groups flew up into the sky above the mountain of God. Once each group reached their desired altitude, they began to fly in a circle. More and more angels joined them from the throne room until the sky was thick with them. It looked like a giant umbrella spinning round and round.

When all the angels were joined to the circle, they began to spin off and leave until they were all gone. After seeing such a majestic event, one would naturally wonder, to what major event are these angels headed to do battle. And then they were here!

Two large angels appeared in my office. They stood like guards. There were angels everywhere! They were down here for battle, for spiritual warfare. There was such a sense of security. Our families, homes, and the business were all protected. The demons couldn't even come close.

There were angels everywhere!

God gave us a mission. My brother in the Lord and I were to go down to a New Age center in our town, which was actually a world-renowned New Age religion center. We were led by the Spirit to stand in front of it and observe the glory of the Lord. These angels were here to do battle, to tear down the stronghold of Satan. All we had to do was stand and be witnesses of God. The enemy knew what was coming and was afraid. They had good reason to be afraid. The battle was to take place at 3:00 p.m.

I went home for lunch and as I prepared to leave, I looked out the front window and saw them in the spirit. Angels were standing around our property like a hedge. They were shoulder to shoulder, facing out, with their swords drawn and pointed upward. I walked around the house and they were all around the yard, on the property line, forming an impenetrable line with their swords flaming like fire.

Meanwhile, down at the oceanfront, the enemy demons were gathering at the New Age devil's den. They were forming a wall. Layer after layer of demons were stacked one upon another. The grounds in front of the place were covered in red. The wall was as high as the building, and the space between the wall and the building was being solidly packed with demons.

The demons were pouring out of the meditation room on the third floor, down to the ground and up the wall, filling the space between the wall and the building for their protection. There was a big red demon inside the place sending these demons out, spewing them out of his mouth, and they were scared. There were big demons and little demons. The big ones were screaming at the little ones to shut up and get in place.

The big ones were fierce looking. The small ones were scared as if it were their first battle. It will be their worst battle. They were preparing their defense and strengthening themselves. We noticed that they had surrounded the place. At the four corners of the wall were some of the strongest, meanest looking demons I had ever seen. On top of the building, right in the middle, was a red dragon! He was ugly, covered in scales, and had fire coming out of his mouth! Never had I seen a more formidable sight. However, these angels and the power of God would crack them open.

Good and evil were facing down each other with a song!

The demons that formed the wall had linked arms and were singing an evil song. "Strong…hold…strong hold…strong…hold." Over and over they sing. Some of the smaller demons weren't singing, so the bigger demons smacked them over the head and told them to sing. They screamed, "Grip! Hold tight and sing!"

The angels had a song of their own. All around me they were singing, "We are the army of the Lord. We are the army! We are the army! We are the army of the Lord!" And so they sang over and over again. What a sound to hear both refrains at the same time. Good and evil were facing down each other and meeting the challenge with a song!

The angels were anxious and ready for battle. They were charged, fired up, and ready to go. At 3:00 p.m. we arrived at the site of the battle. The battle scene was just as the Lord had revealed to us in the Spirit. The demons had made a wall around the perimeter of their grounds, and were joined with linked arms and singing stronghold. There were four big, giant demons, one at each corner of the wall. They were the cornerstones of their defense.

That big red dragon of a demon was on top of the building, for we could see his ugly head. Across the street and looking on, were the forces of the Lord. Archangel Michael was standing, facing the middle of the stronghold, with multitudes of angels on either side and behind him.

We remember the words of the Lord, *"No weapon that is formed against thee shall prosper."*[1] We parked a block from the building where this showdown was taking place, walked across the street facing the center of the stronghold, and stood where the Lord told us to stand. We prayed and bound the evil spirits in the name of Jesus, in the name of the Lamb. We could feel the power of the Holy Spirit build up within us like a boiling steam engine ready to explode!

Suddenly, at the direction of the Spirit, I yelled at the top of my lungs, "Now!" At that moment the angels went in like a flood.

The angels knocked out the biggest demons on the four corners first. Then, like curtains that had come loose from their rods, the walls collapsed and fell straight down. The angels surrounded the place quickly and herded all the demons inside. Simultaneously, the archangel Michael took two giant steps and was on top of the building. With his feet spread wide, he leaned over, grabbed that dragon by the head, and wrapped a big gold chain around its muzzle, sealing its mouth shut. He continued wrapping the chain around its entire body, then dragged it down and threw it into a hole underneath the building.

Angels went down every hallway in the building, through every aisle of their demonic library, and rounded up every demon there. Standing in the library was a big demon holding their book of the dead tightly to his chest. Two angels grabbed him, wrapped him in chains, and put him in that pit—book and all. The angels bound every demon and put them down in the pit with the big dragon demon.

The Lord explained that demons had come from all over

town for this battle. They had come from every hellhole, every place that demons dwell, to be in this battle. The devil himself did not show up for the fight, and the demons were wondering what had happened. They were confused, and even the big red dragon wondered why the devil hadn't come to help them.

As Michael stood on top of the building above their prayer room, there was an explosion of blinding light. The fire of the Holy Spirit came down from heaven into Michael's sword, through his body, and down into the building, permeating every single inch of that place. The light of God shined out of every window of the building.

The light of God shined out of every window.

Then the archangel Michael, standing on top of the building, faced us and the angels all around us and shouted with a loud voice, "It is finished!" The whole event only took about six minutes. A few seconds to defeat them and the rest of the time for clean-up. The enemy was whipped before the battle even began, and now they were in a dark, cold pit.

The angel of the Lord went down to the pit under the building where all those demons were imprisoned and placed a seal over the top. It looked like a steel door, or cover, with the seal of God embossed on top. It cannot be opened until God allows.

We left the battlefield and drove along the oceanfront sensing relief, peace, and an absence of demonic activity. No demons were to be found anywhere! They were all in the pit! Hallelujah!

The Lord allowed us to see what was happening in the spiritual realm as we prayed our simple prayer from the natural realm. There is so much that happens in the spiritual realm. We Christians never know the full extent of the battles, yet they are happening on our behalf. These battles do happen and we are part of them. We sense it and feel it as we pray, but the Lord spares us the horror of the fight. He fights the battle for us.

We need to realize that in the realm of the Spirit, battles of all kinds rage on our behalf. These battles are real, serious, and have consequences that play out in the natural, in our lives. This is not a game! But glory to God, we have One who knows and fights our battles for us, the Lord Jesus Himself, the King of all the armies of heaven!

A word of warning: If the enemy can't win, he'll try to confuse, distract, and weaken your spiritual life, and subsequently your fellowship in the Spirit. One technique he uses is as old as time, "If we can't beat them, we'll join them." We call this an "add-on." After you receive a word from the Holy Spirit, the evil spirits will try to "add on" confusing information, false or half-truths, in order to water down or stop what the Holy Spirit gave you.

For example, the Holy Spirit may reveal a future blessing to encourage you, then the enemy spirit will "add on" a specific date. When the blessing or event doesn't happen on or by that date, you doubt the prophecy and dismiss it in unbelief. Some have given up on their promise and destiny by such tricks of the enemy.

This is another reason to do as it is written in the Bible, *"Beloved, believe not every spirit, but try the spirits whether they are of God."*[2] This is where a lot of people get in trouble. They are truly shown something from the Lord, but the evil spirits add on to what the Holy Spirit shows. If we don't try the spirits under the blood of Jesus, bad information will confuse us or send us off in a wrong direction, in error.

Another rule of thumb is, if the revelation brings glory to you instead of to Jesus, watch out. Something is wrong. The Holy Spirit will always glorify Jesus. We will decrease so that He can increase. Please understand that none of us are perfect.

We are all susceptible to deception.

    Yes, even I have been deceived. I am not the wisest, smartest man with the most discernment. I have had to grow, learn, and sit at the feet of the Master, both then and now. I have believed a false prophesy before. Once, the enemy deceived me into fearing a prophecy of doom. After agonizing over it, the Lord spoke to me, almost in a chuckle, and said, "Don't you know My voice by now?" Immediately I was flooded with peace. I had to learn to discern the spirits. They are slick and so we must try them, to see if they are of God. I can't stress this fact enough. And you know the Lord doesn't mind at all. He has big shoulders and can handle being checked out.

Chapter 17

Intercession

Most Christians engage in spiritual warfare while praying for others. It could be at an altar at church, or with a co-worker at the job, but no matter where you are on this earth, realize that the battle rages in the spiritual realm simultaneously. Books have been written about prayer and intercessory prayer and they're good; but remember, when you put your hands on someone to pray, you enter an arena to fight, to do battle in the name of the Lord.

Don't ever take it lightly. Recognize the seriousness of what you're doing—and for heaven's sake be prepared. Go through the steps to effective prayer, as described in Chapter 8, beforehand if possible. As Paul wrote to Timothy, *"Be prepared in season and out of season."*[1] Compassionately pray for people. Be firm when dealing with the enemy.

Allow Christ in you to rise up through the Holy Spirit and do the work for you. Remember, His hands are within your hands. His feet are within your feet. And His words come out of your mouth. You provide the clean temple, and He works from within you. The battle is the Lord's! This is illustrated by the battles just described. All I had to do was to be obedient and show up, and the Lord Jesus and the Holy Spirit did the fighting for me. I was privileged to stand and see the glory of the Lord.

Much has been written and taught about intercession by wonderful men and women of God, so I will not cover the subject exhaustively here. Suffice it to say that the Lord Jesus is our perfect and supreme example of one who prayed in intercession. We can only imagine what He went through in the wilderness and in the garden. I had a small taste of it when the Holy Spirit taught me about intercession in the Spirit.

It was the day after Christmas, and I began to feel a little ill. Out of the blue, my stomach started cramping and I couldn't get any relief, so I went to the bedroom and lay down on the bed. My stomach was in knots. I prayed to the Lord to touch my body and heal my sickness, and as I prayed, I went into the Spirit. As I asked the Lord to help me, He gave me a vision.

I saw a man. He had dark, medium-length straight hair with medium-length sideburns. He looked sort of familiar but I couldn't place him. He was on an airplane; he had just walked forward from the rear of the plane and sat in a seat by a window on the left side of the plane. My vantage point was from the floor looking up at his face.

He had a concerned look on his face as he looked out of the window. The sky was dark with clouds and a bright, almost full moon became exposed as clouds separated. The moon was traveling fast, back into the clouds again. It was like watching time-lapse photography of the moon traveling through the night sky.

This all seemed strange because I was praying for myself to be healed, and now I have the urge to pray for this man in a vision. I didn't know if he was in danger, or if he was sick. But whatever the problem, I began to pray and intercede for him. I was still sick, curled up in pain, but as I prayed for myself, my prayers turned to intercession for him.

As I prayed in the Spirit, the Lord allowed me to see, through this man's eyes, what he was seeing. For a few moments, I felt like I was sitting in the plane looking out the window and looking at what he was seeing from his perspective. He was sitting above the wing, as I could see it out the window. In front of the wing I could see the ground below and at this point in the flight it appeared that they were at a very low altitude, much lower than a commercial airliner would fly. It was more like the altitude that a small plane would fly. I could even hear the sounds of the plane, the hum of the engines and the sound of the air rushing by.

The ground below was partially covered in snow, and nearby was a small body of water. It was a very solitary moment, alone on that plane, looking out at the night sky as we flew over a cold winter's earth below; the sounds of the plane resounded in my head. I didn't know how to pray for him. Was there going to be a plane crash? Should I pray for his soul?

So I prayed for his safety and his soul, if he didn't know the Lord. As I prayed I had the impression that God did have His hand on this man, and understands the pressure that's going to be on him as he tries to do the right thing. He will have to take a stand in order to do the right thing, whatever that is.

This is a very pressure-filled time in his life, and as for me, I would not want to be in his shoes. If the pressure he feels in his stomach were like the knots I feel in my stomach, then I would not want to be him.

Then, a strange thing happened. My attention had completely turned to praying for him and not myself; and as I finished, I realized that my pain and my sickness had disappeared just as suddenly as it had begun. I was healed! As a matter of fact, I was never really sick!

The Lord had called me to intercessory prayer, spiritual

warfare on behalf of this stranger. I was so identified with him that I literally felt his pain! There is a level of intercessory prayer that identifies you with whom you are praying for. The deeper the intercession, the more you feel their pain or whatever they are experiencing. This is real blood and guts warfare, not for the faint of heart or spiritually weak.

The stronger we are in Christ, the more we can be used of the Lord to fight. This is also a calling. God doesn't just put this on someone. He will train you and groom you for this in stages. But if you are willing, this is an important ministry of the Lord. Brother E.M. Bounds wrote extensively on the subject of intercessory prayer, and I wholeheartedly recommend reading his books. Even if a person doesn't feel "called" to an intercessory prayer ministry, it's an important part of Christian life, so don't be afraid, just do it.

As a footnote to this experience, the next morning I got up and anxiously went to the newspaper to see if there had been a plane crash the night before. Was the man I prayed for in a crash and did he survive? Looking for any news, I found nothing. Thank the Lord. However, there was a picture of the man from my vision. Chill bumps ran all over me as I realized that this man was in fact the new governor-elect of our state. Now I know why he looked familiar in my vision.

The Holy Spirit let me feel what the man was feeling, and had me pray for him in intercessory prayer. My stomach hurt like his until God heard and answered my prayer. I continued to pray for this man throughout his term as our governor.

God's Armor

In the book of Ephesians, the apostle Paul gave instruction for spiritual warfare preparation. Read the following carefully:

Finally, let the Lord make you strong. Depend on his mighty power. Put on all of God's armor. Then you can stand firm against the devil's evil plans. Our fight is not against human beings. It is against the rulers, the authorities and the powers of this dark world. It is against the spiritual forces of evil in the heavenly world. So put on all of God's armor. Evil days will come. But you will be able to stand up to anything. And after you have done everything you can, you will still be standing. So stand firm. Put the belt of truth around your waist. Put the armor of godliness on your chest. Wear on your feet what will prepare you to tell the good news of peace. Also, pick up the shield of faith. With it you can put out all of the flaming arrows of the evil one. Put on the helmet of salvation. And take the sword of the Holy Spirit. The sword is God's word. At all times, pray by the power of the Spirit. Pray all kinds of prayers. Be watchful, so that you can pray. Always keep on praying for all of God's people.[2]

One day a brother approached me in a hallway at church with a problem. He was disturbed by a dream he had the night before. He described that in his dream he was standing, wearing his armor, and it was in terrible shape. It was rusty, dented, soiled, and all beat up. He wanted to know what the dream meant. Immediately, the Holy Spirit quickened me with the interpretation of the dream. I told him, "The problem is that you are wearing *your* armor. If we try to fight our spiritual battles with only our armor, we will end up being beaten and defeated as you saw yourself in your dream. We are to put on *God's* armor. Then when the enemy sees us in His armor, he knows Christ is inside and we can't be beaten."

Through study and prayer, the Lord continued to teach me that the pieces of armor as described above in Paul's writings are actually attributes of God. Keeping ourselves in fellowship with Father, Lord Jesus, and the Holy Spirit, and decreasing self as They increase within us keeps us strong, able to defend ourselves against enemy attacks, and to fight the spiritual battles that are ordained of God.

In the Bible, God instructed man to subdue the earth and gave him dominion over every living thing that moves upon the earth.[3] That is our daily test, to subdue the earth, to subdue our part of the earth, our sphere of influence. With men this is impossible, but with God all things are possible. It is actually Christ in us who subdues. We stand in His authority as His servants. He may send His angels to fight spiritual battles with and for us, or He may show up in person. The Holy Spirit directs our prayers of intercession. We are to be Christ-like, following His example and being humble servants—not arrogant warriors. The enemy doesn't easily surrender power or authority on this earth; but Christ, yes the same Christ who is in us, has all authority and power on earth, heaven, and everywhere.

When we enter into spiritual warfare, we are not alone, ever.

When we enter into spiritual warfare, we are not alone, ever. He is with us and actually fights our battles for us! We had just had a tremendous victory in a community outreach where many people came to Jesus. Afterward, while praying in the Spirit, I found myself in what looked like a dark room. In the distance, about twenty yards away, and to my right, I saw the silhouette of a man walking.

I could hear the sound of his heels, *click, click, click,* on the hard floor as he came in my direction. He came from my right and it looked like he might walk on by until he was in front of me, then he abruptly turned left headed directly toward me. He walked right up to my face.

It was the devil himself! I can never remember this kind of confrontation with him before this. He got right in my face and said, "How dare you intrude in my business! How dare you intrude into my territory!" He began to let me have it. I remember those eyes; I've never seen such hate. I found myself shrinking back as he lambasted me. Just as I was feeling intimidated, Jesus rose up behind and around me.

It was like I had shrunk into Jesus as He rose up around me. I felt protected as He looked the devil in the eyes and said, "Back off! I am the one in control. I am the one doing this!" With that, the devil took a couple of steps back, bowed his head, bowed at the waist and backed off, literally. In that bowed position, he walked backward the same way he walked in. And he did it hurriedly. To a mere mortal the enemy can be intimidating, but to Jesus, he's nothing. No contest.

The Lord reminded me that we have a responsibility to pray and intercede for our family and those for whom He has given us to pray. Jesus said, "You can't do passive battle, Son. Spiritual warfare takes guts, determination, perseverance, wisdom, strength, and a willingness to never give up. What is loosed in heaven is loosed on earth. What is bound in heaven is bound on earth. Come here, in the Spirit, to this place in heaven and bind and loose. The devils are not afraid of a man who knows My name, but they are terrified of a man who walks in the Spirit. Walk in the Holy Spirit!"

Pray for the Lord to open your eyes to see your spiritual warfare. Ask Him, and according to His will for you, He'll do it.

Chapter 18

Church Fellowship

The church, the glorious bride of Christ! Oh how the Master loves His church, His people. And oh, how the enemy tries to destroy the church and every member. Having spent most of my life in church, I have seen the glorious and the ugly side of church. It's only natural that people judge the church by their own experience or the experience of a friend or family member. And if a person judges the church only by what they see on television, then their understanding could really be twisted away from the truth.

I know what it's like to be hurt by people in the church. I've been hurt, disappointed, and disillusioned by the church. Fortunately, I've had a deep, personal relationship with the Lord Jesus, so I never lost my faith in Him, only in some people and a few leaders. The longer I live, the more I understand that no person, no pastor, and no church is perfect. Some people hop from church to church looking for that perfect church and never find it.

I've known people who stay in the same church their whole lives and are just as frustrated and disappointed. Without the love of the Lord, a church can become like a civic organization, full of good works, yet devoid of the gospel. Other churches become religious political organizations that foster pastoral power and enrichment on the backs of the people, and are run by men full of personal ambition for career advancement at any cost.

Yet most churches are good, filled with good people and good pastors whose only goal and ambition is to see people saved, the gospel proclaimed, and the name of Jesus lifted up. The church does triumph in spite of the tricks and strategies of the enemy to destroy it. However, there are millions of people across the country who are church refugees. These people are favorable to, and actually love God and the Lord Jesus, yet want nothing to do with the church, primarily because they've been hurt by the institution, the pastor, or someone in the church.

They must be reached with the love of Jesus and the love of His church. We need to assemble together so that the Lord can manifest Himself to us and through us to each other, and to a hurting world. But even with all the ups and downs, the church is special to the Lord and is His most cherished possession.

Several years ago, after I began walking in the Spirit, the Holy Spirit did a work of healing in me. He showed me a very deep hurt within me. It was a hurt with the church. As a young man just starting out in ministry, my pastor betrayed and tried to destroy me. I discovered through the Holy Spirit that this hurt was far deeper than I ever imagined, even many years later.

It hurt my spirit to the core and caused a wall to come between the church and me. I sobbed and cried as God brought that out of me. In that place deep inside, where I held hurt for the church, God healed me and put a love for the church where the hurt had been. He put the church within me! He admonished me to never take His church lightly. As I lay on the floor like a limp dishrag, God gave me a vision of the church.

I saw many church buildings, and they were burning with fire on top. I saw myself at a pulpit preaching; and as I was preaching, the church ceiling was on fire above me. All I could see were the lost souls sitting in the church. There were sinners among the saints, and I could see that they were going to hell, and it grieved my heart. I found myself worrying about them and their lost condition. The Holy Spirit in me was grieving for those lost souls in the church. I became curled up in the fetal position in the floor in great pain. This burden for lost souls hurt me so badly. I cried out, "Oh Lord, save them! Save them!" And then I would tell the devil, "Stay away from them. They're mine!"

"Oh Lord, save them! Save them!"

I battled for lost souls in prayer for some time. It was a battle that came from the deepest part of my soul. The next thing I knew, I looked straight ahead and saw what at first looked like a hole in the wall. Looking closer I realized it was an elevator, with the door open and no floor. Whoever stepped in would fall down the shaft…to hell!

It was a big doorway to hell and masses of people were going in. Some were going in face first, some were tumbling in, and some were falling in backward, reaching out for help as they disappeared into the very depths of despair. It grieved me that they were going into hell. It was terrifying. I tried to save them, but I couldn't. I reached out, but couldn't reach them. I tried to grab hold of them, but couldn't. There were so many of them, and they were all lost. I'll never forget the terrified looks on their faces. I struggled and was able to save a few from falling, but the vast majority was lost and there was nothing I could do about it.

The Holy Spirit screamed, "No! No! No!" He was so outraged that they were going to hell. During this vision, I was stretched out across the floor, reaching for the people falling into the doorway to hell. It felt like God was holding me by the ankles to keep me from falling into the pit myself, as I stretched to reach people.

I have never forgotten this vision, as it was so real and terrifying. At the time, I thought of those people as lost souls, people of the world who didn't know Christ. Maybe they had never heard the name of Christ. It was a motivation to spread the gospel. But looking back now and thinking about the vision, I have come to a new and even more chilling understanding of what the Lord was trying to show me. These people were the lost who sit in church! Oh my Lord! No wonder the Holy Spirit was screaming no! These people had attended church, sat among believers, and knew better.

Sitting in a church service week after week, even being a member of a church won't save you. We must have a personal relationship with Lord Jesus to be saved from hell. Church membership and religion are not enough. We must repent to the Lord and say, "Lord Jesus, I ask You into my life. I want to turn from living my life under my own control. Come now and live Your life in me. Cleanse me from my sins. I receive You as my Lord and my Savior. I will live for You and serve You all the days of my life. In Jesus' name, amen."

I have prayed that prayer with hundreds of people. When you pray and receive Christ as your personal Savior, a new life begins. Your old self is gone—God makes you new from the inside out. You become part of His church and part of Him!

Small Groups

One day my brother in the Lord and I were in the Spirit walking together in heaven when we came to a short wall, one you could sit on if you wanted. We stepped up on it and walked over onto a grassy meadow. On my left was the forest. Straight ahead was a large meadow where people were sitting around in small groups, as if they were having picnics. There were little groups of people sitting around, talking and conversing all over this meadow.

In the distance beyond the large meadow was the city of God. It looked so magnificent that mere words cannot describe it properly. It had architectural features that have never been seen on earth. Colors and light shone out of the city, causing it to sparkle like a jewel, a sparkling city on a hill.

Well, my brother and I decided to walk over and sit among this one group of maybe seven to nine people who were sitting on the ground talking. We were welcomed to sit down with them and listen. We couldn't understand what they were saying, as they were speaking in a foreign or heavenly language. As we sat down, the main person speaking looked over and acknowledged us warmly. God interpreted for us. He said, "Welcome." Then he told the group, "These are the spirits of two prophets of the Lord, in training."

Then a sister on my right handed me a piece of fruit. I took it, bit into it, tasted it, chewed it, swallowed it, and it was absolutely heavenly! I didn't want it to end. It was like a watermelon and banana combined. It had a very nice, sweet taste to it. My brother and I ate fruit and savored it. So help me we could taste it in our physical bodies. We stayed with the group for a while, and then we left and continued walking in the Spirit through heaven.

The Lord revealed to me that this group wasn't composed of saints who had died on earth and were now living in heaven. No, they were people on earth in a small cell group, fellowshipping in the Spirit together! The Lord allowed us to witness and be part of their experience in this place.

This is just one of many times when my brother in the Lord and I have had visions together. As a matter of fact, several of the visions I've shared in this book were actually joint visions. As we walk in the Spirit together, at the Holy Spirit's discretion, we are able to share in visions together. Our physical bodies are here on earth while our spirits walk in the heavenly realms together. There are times when more than two of us share in a vision together. I have experienced this many times.

Don't limit God. Remember what Jesus said, *"For where two or three come together in my name, there am I with them."* [1] Which also means to us that if we're together in unity in the Spirit of Christ, under the anointing of the Holy Spirit, Christ is there in the midst of us and He'll show us things and take us places. If we're in unity and under the anointing then we can all, whether it's two, three, or three thousand, go together and live out of heaven, and experience the heavenly mysteries of God in Christ!

This is so exciting! It puts a new depth to the Scriptures and to what being in Christ means to us. I know that as I gaze out upon this earth, Christ is looking at this earth though my eyes. And as Jesus looks around in heaven, I'm looking at heaven through His eyes! Now He is with us and we are with Him.

Jesus prayed to Father, *"Father, I want those you have given me to be with me where I am, and to see my glory, the glory you have given me because you loved me before the creation of the world."* [2] Sure we know that when we die and go to heaven we'll see Him, but He wants us to experience heaven now, in this life here on earth. Christ is calling His church to a new and special intimacy with Him, with Father and the Holy Spirit.

The Bible tells us that, *"God is spirit, and his worshipers must worship in spirit and in truth."* [3] While in the Spirit, Lord Jesus came to me and said, "Worship me in spirit and in truth. This means to worship me with your spirit, in the

Spirit. To worship in truth means to worship in righteousness, to live right. When you live right and do right, you worship Me. Worship me in spirit and in truth."

To do what the Lord commands is really not hard; it's obedience with great reward. Let me share a few more experiences of what it's like to fellowship in the Spirit with the Lord as a church, with a small group of believers.

In one meeting, the glory of God descended on us and we were taken to the heavenly realm, before the throne of God. We all worshipped Him before the throne in spirit and in truth. As I lay on my face before the throne in heaven, Father came down and put His arms around me, hugged me, and loved me with unconditional love. My arms dropped to my sides, as I couldn't contain myself. In the flesh, I lay on the floor and cried as, in the Spirit, Father was holding me and loving me like the Father I needed. It was as if I had always known Him, and yet, at the same time, like I had never known Him.

Another time Father appeared before me. He stood directly in front of me, facing me, and held my hands. As He looked into my eyes, I could hear Him talking to me although with His mouth, He wasn't saying a word. It seemed to come out of His eyes. My natural mind couldn't understand it, but in my spirit I felt His overpowering love. We stood there for a few moments and He simply loved me.

Over His shoulder I could see my brother in the Lord with Jesus, sitting on a bench. Father and I walked over to the bench and sat down beside them. To my left on the bench sat, Father, Lord Jesus, and my brother in the Lord, in that order. Then it changed, and it seemed like we had all changed positions, then we changed positions again, all without moving.

Before we knew it we couldn't tell where one of us began and the other ended. We were all one! We were one in all, in each other, as we sat on that bench. We experienced each other's thoughts. Not that my brother and I were God, we were just totally meshed with Father, Lord Jesus, and the Holy Spirit. All five of us were one, and the Lord let us stay that way all day!

Unity in Fellowship

There's no higher expression of love that the Lord can give. To be in complete unity with God: the Father, Lord Jesus, and the Holy Spirit. To be all in all with them in Their love is the ultimate spiritual experience. In the past, we have had revelations of the different aspects of Their personalities, but because of where we are in them, we are experiencing aspects of all three personalities, simultaneously. We see the exuberance of the Holy Spirit, the aura and glory of Father, and the companionship and love of Jesus, all at once. Hallelujah!

On a different night, we began our meeting with six of us. It seemed like Father just walked into the room as we prayed, and we all received a touch from the Master. Lord Jesus opened the spiritual eyes of everyone there who had not seen in the Spirit. The Holy Spirit's presence was in the room so strongly that I was slain, lost in the Spirit most of the evening, just lying on the floor. Everyone prayed for one another, giving prophecies and also being slain. Being slain means you lay down and you appear asleep or dead, although sometimes you can still hear what's going on around you.

It seems like we all had a vision together, with each person seeing part of it, and then overlapping with another person's part. One brother saw a stairway coming down what looked like a pyramid. On the bottom of the steps at the foot of the pyramid was Gabriel, the archangel, holding a trumpet and looking over his right shoulder up to the top of the steps waiting for the signal to blow his horn.

He also saw a giant valve being opened, and out of the

spigot were all sorts of confusion, and vile things. My spirit saw it as the wrath of God. When it opened, there was a burst of light that came out first, then the junk. At the same time, another brother saw a flash, a wave of fire that came across the whole earth. Then I saw Jesus with the crown of many crowns on His head, sitting on His white horse. Two other brothers saw a room with many robes. One brother saw us all in a cloakroom being handed beautiful white robes by angels. After we each put on our robe, we walked down a long corridor lined with angels.

We had been with the Lord, and were in one mind and one accord. We didn't want to leave the place. After it was over, like so many times before after being in the presence of God, we all stood outside, looking at each other, looking at the sky, marveling at the things He had done. And yet at the same time having great anticipation for what is yet to come.

Time after time, in meeting after meeting, the Lord ministered to us in a powerful way. It was common for there to be laying room only on the floor, because that is where we spent most of the meeting, on the floor. We would pray in the Spirit together for hours, receiving blessings individually and as a group. And it was typical to linger afterward, first inside, and then outside in the parking lot by the cars. Sometimes the power of God lingered with us outside, and people would be slain and blessed in the parking lot. Oh what a glorious time!

This is the next great move of God for His church. I've said it before and I'll say it again. He wants to fellowship with His children and open their eyes to see Him! It's hard to explain everything that happens in these meetings because there's so much.

The Lord demonstrated how we can fellowship in the Spirit seeing the same things at the same time. It's wonderful to be in God's will, to help people, and fellowship with other people in the same mind in one accord under the power and anointing of the Holy Spirit. The Holy Spirit ministered to each of us through each of us. We prayed for one another, sang, and worshipped with our arms linked together, standing in a semicircle swaying in the Spirit.

> *His intent was that now, through the church, the manifold wisdom of God should be made known to the rulers and authorities in the heavenly realms, according to his eternal purpose which he accomplished in Christ Jesus our Lord. In him and through faith in him we may approach God with freedom and confidence."*[4]

We have seen and experienced this Scripture. This relationship is certainly God's will for His church. There have been times when the realm of heaven was so real that a portal was opened here on earth for us. Imagine walking to a part of the building where the power of the Holy Spirit was so strong that just standing in that spot transported you, in the Spirit, to a place in heaven such as the waterfall previously mentioned. Or another spot in the building where you find yourself standing in the throne room of God, with the twenty-four elders, then and cast your crown before Christ. Well, it has happened to us!

This is a significant development! Heaven and earth merged in the Spirit. Everyone experienced this as they went from place to place in our warehouse; it was like walking around in heaven. I believe the Lord is pouring out His Spirit in a way that is different from any other time in history. He is giving us a seed, an example of what He wants to do, and will do on the earth in these last days.

The power of God has been so strong upon me that there were occasions when I've seen the Lord Jesus in the Spirit, and then He appeared to my natural eye. He and the Holy Spirit and Father have appeared to me so strongly that it seemed I was seeing Them with my natural eyes. Only they know if it was spiritual or natural, but for me it doesn't matter when it's so strong that I can't tell the difference, I just marvel in Their presence. Hallelujah!

Merging into Heaven

The closer to the time of His coming, the more of heaven we'll sense around us until, if it were possible, we would be in heaven and not here! There have been times that, as we worshipped the Lord, the sound of a mighty rushing wind blew through our meeting as the Holy Ghost fell on us in a mighty way.

When you worship Him in Spirit and in truth, there are sacred times of ultimate holiness, and there are also times of lighthearted laughter and joy. There are times when the Holy Spirit, Father, or Lord Jesus would say something funny and we'd all burst out into holy laughter. And the more we laughed, the more He laughed. Times like this are priceless and special.

After reading about these things some may ask, "So what? Whatever came of such a powerful move of God? Praying and having wonderful experiences are good, but what about the here and now? Are we so heavenly minded that we're no earthly good?" Good questions. I'm glad you asked. I'd love to brag on the Lord.

One day two of my sisters in the Lord were led to go into the inner city projects and witness. Well, these witnessing visits turned into much more. They decided to have a picnic for souls. We all joined together (all twelve of us) and gathered up some food, clothes, and BBQ grills and headed out to the projects.

On a hot, beautiful Saturday morning we sang, preached, fed, and led seventy-five precious souls to the Lord. We continued these events, which I called Love Feasts. Over the next four years we had several Love Feasts around the area. More than 762 volunteer workers from 150 churches helped us feed more than 11,700 people, distribute more than 61,100 pounds of food, give out truckloads of clothes, and lead 888 men, women, and children to accept Jesus Christ as their personal Savior!

Lord Jesus also gave me the idea to start a food ministry, Tidewater Foodwagon. We collected and delivered more than a million pounds of food in our local area during this same period of time. This has been documented and awards have been given in appreciation. How we did it I can't explain. It was just a sovereign act of God.

Our little group grew, and one night we had to expand our chapel space. The Holy Spirit reminded me of the time when He told me, "Make a place where I can flow and I will build it." Well, He is welcomed to flow here and He does. The Lord is touching people one life at a time. This is more important than any elaborate program we could come up with. There are no fancy speeches, no professional singing or overhead projection, and nothing it takes to have a modern-day church. All these things are nice, but they aren't needed!

All we need is a modest place like a corner in an old warehouse and hearts that are willing to be touched by the Spirit of God. All we need are hearts that welcome the Spirit of God, the Spirit of peace and life to come in and have fellowship with us. Our prayer is, "*Lord, open our spiritual eyes and let us see Your glory and have fellowship with You,* **Spirit fellowship**."

NOTES

Introduction

1. 1 Corinthians 13:12

2. Ephesians 1:17-18

Chapter 1: Drawn by Hunger

1. See John 14:6

2. Psalm 42:1-2

3. John 1:1

4. 1 Corinthians 12:7

5. 1 Thessalonians 5:17

6. Joel 2:28-30

Chapter 2: The Timeless Realm of God

1. See Mark 10:27

2. Psalm 41:13

3. Psalm 93:2

4. Hebrews 1:8

5. Hebrews 13:8

6. Exodus 3:14

7. John 1:1-2

8. Revelation 22:13

9. John 8:58

10. 1 John 1:9

11. James 4:14

12. John 3:16

13. John 6:47

14. John 10:10

15. John 17:24

16. John 16:13-14

Chapter 3: The Trinity of One

1. 1 John 5:7 KJV

2. Matthew 11:19 KJV

3. James 2:23

4. Genesis 1:1 KJV

5. Ephesians 4:4-6

6. 1 Corinthians 8:6

7. Hebrews 1:8

8. Acts 5:3-4

9. 1 Corinthians 11:3

10. 2 John 1:3

11. John 14:16-17 KJV

12. Genesis 3:22

13. John 17:11

14. John 17:21-23

15. Genesis 1:26

16. Genesis 1:27

17. Proverbs 20:27 KJV

18. 1 Corinthians 12:13

19. 1 Corinthians 12:12
20. 1 Corinthians 12:27
21. 1 John 1:5-7
22. Matthew 17:2
23. 2 Corinthians 3:18
24. See Matthew chapter17.
25. John 17:22-23
26. John 17:21
27. Exodus 3:2

Chapter 4: The Three Faces of God

1. 1 Chronicles 16:11
2. 2 Chronicles 7:14
3. Psalm 31:16
4. Revelation 3:8
5. Exodus 20:21-22
6. 1 Kings 8:12
7. See 1 John 1:5
8. 1 John 4:12
9. 1 John 1:1-4
10. Genesis 32:30
11. Exodus 24:9-11
12. Exodus 33:11
13. Acts 7:56
14. Exodus 33:18
15. Jeremiah 33:3
16. Ephesians 1:17-18

17. Mark 11:24

Chapter 5: The Mystery of the Gospel

1. Colossians 1:26-27
2. Mark 4:11 KJV
3. Ephesians 1:17-19
4. Romans 5:12
5. 1 Corinthians 15:21-22
6. Genesis 2:8
7. Isaiah 14:14
8. Romans 3:10-13
9. 2 Corinthians 4:4
10. Ephesians 2:12
11. Galatians 4:4
12. Hebrews 2:14
13. Romans 5:8
14. Romans 5:19
15. 2 Corinthians 5:21

Chapter 6: Jesus in My Mirror

1. Romans 6:3-8
2. Romans 8:16-17
3. 1 Corinthians 15:21-22
4. Galatians 2:20
5. Colossians 2:9-13
6. Colossians 3:1-3
7. 1 Corinthians 13:12
8. 2 Corinthians 3:18

9. Colossians 3:4

10. Romans 8:10-11

11. 1 Corinthians 6:17

12. 1 Corinthians 15:21-22

13. 2 Corinthians 4:18

14. 2 Corinthians 5:17

15. Ephesians 2:10

16. Ephesians 4:24

17. Colossians 3:10

18. 1 Thessalonians 5:23

19. 1 Corinthians 1:30

20. 1 Corinthians 3:16

21. Galatians 3:26-27

22. Galatians 2:20

23. Matthew 18:20

24. John 17:20-26

Chapter 7: Effective Prayer

1. James 5:16

2. 1 Thessalonians 5:23

3. 1 Thessalonians 4:4

4. 1 Corinthians 3:16

5. Hebrews 4:12

6. John 4:24

7. Mark 2:8

8. 2 Corinthians 13:14 KJV

9. Hebrews 10:22

10. Hebrews 9:14

11. Matthew 22:37

12. Psalms 84:2

13. Galatians 5:17

14. Hebrews 12:1

Chapter 8 The Steps

1. Hebrews 10:19-20

2. 1 Peter 18:19

3. Colossians 1:19-20

4. Romans 6:6-7

5. Romans 6:3-4

6. Romans 6:11

Chapter 9: Follow Boldly into Heaven

1. Hebrews 4:16 KJV

2. Romans 12:1 KJV

3. Revelation 15:2

4. 1 Thessalonians 5:23

5. Revelation 1:12

6. 1 Kings 7:48

7. 1 John 5:14-15

8. Hebrews 4:14

9. Exodus 25:10-22

10. Revelation 11:19

11. Revelation 7:9-10

12. Ephesians 6:11-18

Chapter 10: Heaven

1. Ephesians 1:18
2. Song of Solomon 4:13-15
3. Psalm 149:1-4
4. Psalm 73:24

Chapter 11: The Beachcomber

1. Psalm 116:15
2. Matthew 18:20

Chapter 12: Our Family Home

1. Revelation 22:1-2

Chapter 13: God Is Light

1. 1 John 1:5-7
2. Job 38:19
3. Psalm 89:15
4. Colossians 1:12
5. 1 Thessalonians 5:5
6. 1 John 1:5

Chapter 14: Angels

1. Isaiah 6:1-3 KJV
2. Revelation 7:11
3. Luke 15:10
4. Luke 2:10-11
5. Matthew 18:10
6. Matthew 13:41

7. Revelation 5:11

8. 2 Peter 2:4

9. 2 Corinthians 11:14-15

10. Colossians 2:18

Chapter 15: Angelic Encounters

1. Hebrews 13:2

Chapter 16: Spiritual Warfare

1. Isaiah 54:17 KJV

2. 1 John 4:1 KJV

Chapter 17: Intercession

1. 2 Timothy 4:2

2. Ephesians 6:10-18 NIRV

3. Genesis 1:28

Chapter 18: Church Fellowship

1. Matthew 18:20

2. John 17:24

3. John 4:24

4. Ephesians 3:10-12

Study Guide

Introduction

1.) Before the fall of man, Adam walked in _____ with God experiencing God's glory with a _____.

2.) Through Jesus, we are born again into the Kingdom of God, but our _____ are not open.

3.) Jesus said "Father, I want those you have given me to be with me where I am, and to _____ my glory." John 17:24

4.) The apostle Paul wrote, "I pray also that the _____ of your heart may be enlightened in order that you may know the hope to which he has called you.

Chapter 1 Drawn by Hunger

1.) With your natural eyes, you see your surroundings in the natural realm. But at the same time, with the _____ of your spirit you see in the spiritual realm. This is called an _____ vision.

2.) The New Testament experience is for believers today. Heaven can be experienced now as we live in two different _____ or two different _____ through our spirit.

CHAPTER 2 THE TIMELESS REALM OF GOD

1.) God lives in the _____, _____, and _____ at the same time!

2.) When God forgives and cleanses us from our sins, they are _____ from the   past.

3.) Since God exists in the _____, and doesn't see our sins, it proves that they are gone.

CHAPTER 3 THE TRINITY OF ONE

1.) God is actually _____ separate personalities, yet one.

2.) Through Christ we are _____ with God.

CHAPTER 4 THE THREE FACES OF GOD

1.) The Holy Spirit is a _____.

2.) The Holy Spirit has a _____ we can see in the spirit.

3.) Moses saw God _____ to face.

CHAPTER 5 THE MYSTERY OF THE GOSPEL

1.) The mystery of the gospel is Christ _____, the hope of glory.

2.) When Adam fell, ____ all fell because we all were ____ him.

3.) In Adam all _____, but in Christ all will be made _____.

CHAPTER 6 JESUS IN MY MIRROR

1.) We were _____ into Jesus Christ.

2.) We were _____ in him, _____ in him, _____ in him, and now we ____ in him.

3.) Focus on the ____ God has given you in Christ.

CHAPTER 7 EFFECTIVE PRAYER

1.) Each person is made up of three parts: _____, _____, and _____.

2.) Our spirit has three main faculties: _____, _____, and _____.

3.) Our soul has three main faculties: _____, _____, and _____.

4.) Our body has five main faculties: _____, _____, _____, _____, and _____.

5.) Plan a _____ of prayer, repentance, and _____ by the _____ of Jesus.

CHAPTER 8 THE STEPS

1.) Ask God to forgive you for every sin, known and

_____.

    2.) Ask Him to destroy the force of _____, in every faculty of your _____, _____, and _____, by the _____ of Jesus.

    3.) We come to the cross for _____.

    4.) We submit every faculty of our tri–part being to Christ in his _____, _____, and _____.

CHAPTER 9 FOLLOW BOLDLY INTO HEAVEN

    1.) We come _____ before the throne of grace.

    2.) We present every faculty of our _____ being as a living _____ on the altar in heaven.

    3.) We present every faculty of our tri-part being to be _____ holy on the sea of glass.

    4.) We enter the Holy Place in heaven and ask for a fresh in-filling of the Holy Spirit at the _____.

    5.) We take communion with the Lord Jesus at the _____.

    6.) We _____ Christ and gain fresh revelation of his word

    7.) We intercede with Christ at the _____.

    8.) We join the Three at the ark in the _____, or throne room.

Study Guide

9.) We put on the full _____ and are ready for spiritual warfare.

Chapter 10 Heaven

1.) The atmosphere in heaven is _____ yet leaves you wanting more.

Chapter 11 The Beachcomber

1.) There are continual _____ in heaven greeted by _____.

2.) Jesus said, "The true religion is to _____, _____, and _____, for me."

Chapter 12 Our Heavenly Home

1.) Our _____ is a place where all family and ancestors dwell.

Chapter 13 God is Light

1.) God is _____.

2.) There is a _____ of light.

3.) The city is inhabited by _____ of light.

Chapter 14 Angels

1.) Angels _____ God's throne.

2.) Angels study and worship the _____ of God

Chapter 15 Angelic Encounters

1.) Never develop a _____ with angels.

2.) You may _____ an angel without realizing.

Chapter 16 Spiritual Warfare

1.) Spiritual warfare is fought in the _____ realm.

2.) Do not be deceived by Angels of light, but _____ the spirits to see if they are from God.

Chapter 17 Intercession

1.) Be _____ in season and out of season.

2.) When we enter into _____ we are never alone.

Chapter 18 Church Fellowship

1.) We need to assemble together so that the Lord can _____ to us, and _____ to each other.

2.) When we, as believers, fellowship together here on earth, we also _____ together in heaven.

Study Guide Key

Introduction

1.) Before the fall of man, Adam walked in <u>fellowship</u> with God experiencing God's glory with a <u>spiritual connection</u>.

2.) Through Jesus, we are born again into the Kingdom of God, but our <u>eyes</u> are not open.

3.) Jesus said "Father, I want those you have given me to be with me where I am, and to <u>see</u> my glory." John 17:24

4.) The apostle Paul wrote, "I pray also that the <u>eyes</u> of your heart may be enlightened in order that you may know the hope to which he has called you.

Chapter 1 Drawn by Hunger

1.) With your natural eyes, you see your surroundings in the natural realm. But at the same time, with the <u>eyes</u> of your spirit you see in the spiritual realm. This is called an <u>open</u> vision.

2.) The New Testament experience is for believers today. Heaven can be experienced now as we live in two different <u>realms</u> or two different <u>lives</u> through our spirit.

Chapter 2 The Timeless Realm of God

1.) God lives in the <u>past</u>, <u>present</u>, and <u>future</u> at the same time!

2.) When God forgives and cleanses us from our sins,

they are <u>purged</u> from the past.

3.) Since God exists in the <u>past</u>, and doesn't see our sins, it proves that they are gone.

Chapter 3 The Trinity of One

1.) God is actually <u>three</u> separate personalities, yet one.

2.) Through Christ we are <u>one</u> with God.

Chapter 4 The Three Faces of God

1.) The Holy Spirit is a <u>person</u>.

2.) The Holy Spirit has a <u>face</u> we can see in the spirit.

3.) Moses saw God <u>face</u> to face.

Chapter 5 The Mystery of the Gospel

1.) The mystery of the gospel is Christ <u>in us</u>, the hope of glory.

2.) When Adam fell, <u>we</u> all fell because we all were <u>in</u> him.

3.) In Adam all <u>die</u>, but in Christ all will be made <u>alive</u>.

Chapter 6 Jesus in My Mirror

1.) We were <u>baptized</u> into Jesus Christ.

2.) We were <u>crucified</u> in him, <u>died</u> in him, <u>raised</u> in him, and now we <u>live</u> in him.

3.) Focus on the <u>life</u> God has given you in Christ.

Chapter 7 Effective Prayer

1.) Each person is made up of three parts: <u>spirit</u>, <u>soul</u>, and <u>body</u>.

2.) Our spirit has three main faculties: <u>intuition</u>, <u>communion</u>, and <u>conscience</u>.

3.) Our soul has three main faculties: <u>mind</u>, <u>will</u>, and <u>emotion</u>.

4.) Our body has five main faculties: <u>sight</u>, <u>hearing</u>, <u>taste</u>, <u>touch</u>, and <u>smell</u>.

5.) Plan a <u>course</u> of prayer, repentance, and <u>cleansing</u> by the <u>blood</u> of Jesus.

CHAPTER 8 THE STEPS

1.) Ask God to forgive you for every sin, known and <u>unknown</u>.

2.) Ask Him to destroy the force of <u>sin</u>, in every faculty of your <u>spirit</u>, <u>soul</u>, and <u>body</u>, by the <u>blood</u> of Jesus.

3.) We come to the cross for <u>deliverance</u>.

4.) We submit every faculty of our tri–part being to Christ in his <u>cross</u>, <u>grave</u>, and <u>resurrection</u>.

CHAPTER 9 FOLLOW BOLDLY INTO HEAVEN

1.) We come <u>boldly</u> before the throne of grace.

2.) We present every faculty of our <u>tri–part</u> being as a living <u>sacrifice</u> on the altar in heaven.

3.) We present every faculty of our tri-part being to be <u>sanctified</u> holy on the sea of glass.

4.) We enter the Holy Place in heaven and ask for a fresh in-filling of the Holy Spirit at the <u>lampstand</u>.

5.) We take communion with the Lord Jesus at the <u>table of shew bread</u>.

6.) We <u>put on</u> Christ and gain fresh revelation of his word

7.) We intercede with Christ at the <u>altar of incense</u>.

8.) We join the Three at the ark in the <u>holy of holies</u>, or throne room.

9.) We put on the full <u>armor of God</u> and are ready for spiritual warfare.

Chapter 10 Heaven

1.) The atmosphere in heaven is <u>satisfying</u> yet leaves you wanting more

Chapter 11 The Beachcomber

1.) There are continual <u>homecomings</u> in heaven greeted by <u>family and friends</u>.

2.) Jesus said, "the true religion is to <u>love me, desire me,</u> and <u>seek me</u>, for me."

Chapter 12 Our Heavenly Home

1.) Our <u>family home</u> is a place where all family and ancestors dwell.

Chapter 13 God is Light

1.) God is <u>light</u>.

2.) There is a <u>city</u> of light.

3.) The city is inhabited by <u>people</u> of light.

Chapter 14 Angels

1.) Angels <u>attend</u> God's throne.

2.) Angels study and worship the <u>attributes</u> of God.

Chapter 15 Angelic Encounters

1.) Never develop a <u>relationship</u> with angels.

2.) You may <u>entertain</u> an angel without realizing.

Chapter 16 Spiritual Warfare

1.) Spiritual warfare is fought in the <u>spiritual</u> realm.

2.) Do not be deceived by Angels of light, but <u>try or test</u> the spirits to see if they are from God.

Chapter 17 Intercession

1.) Be <u>prepared</u> in season and out of season.

2.) When we enter into spiritual warfare we are never alone.

Chapter 18 Church Fellowship

1.) We need to assemble together so that the Lord can <u>manifest Himself</u> to us, and <u>through us</u> to each other.

2.) When we, as believers, fellowship together here on earth, we also <u>fellowship in the Spirit</u> together in heaven.

About the Author

Gene Markland accepted the Lord Jesus as his personal Savior at the age of twelve and received the baptism of the Holy Spirit at the age of seventeen. He followed the Lord's call to ministry at the age of twenty-three and holds ministerial credentials with the Church of God. He followed the path into Street Ministry, Coffee House Ministry, Television Ministry, Food Ministry, large events and concerts, Radio Ministry, and now the Internet. Gene served as a ministry coach on staff at the Christian Broadcasting Network in the National Prayer Center, and is a contributing writer for cbn.com and *The Church Guide*. It has been his joy to preach, teach, and serve as a musician at his local church. Gene is a self-employed business owner. He lives in Virginia Beach, Virginia, with his wife of 42 years, Martha, and their daughter Laura, a graduate of George Mason University.

Gene Markland

PO Box 65007

Virginia Beach, VA 23467

www.spiritfellowship.com

Reading List

A Normal Christian Life by Watchmen Nee

The Spiritual Man by Watchmen Nee

Secrets of the Most Holy Place by Don Nori

Bone of his Bone by FJ Hugo

The Practice of the Presence of God by Brother Lawrence

Within Heavens Gates by Rebecca Springer

The Secret Place by Dr. Dale a Fife

The Seer by James Goll

How to Meet in Homes by Gene Edwards

The Divine Romance by Gene Edwards

God's plan for Man by Finis Dake

Exploring Romans by John Phillips

Renewal Theology Volumes One, Two, and *Three* by Dr. J Rodman Williams

LOVE to READ?

Get FREE eBooks,
Deep Discounts and New Release Updates!
Sign up now.
destinyimage.com/freebooks

SHARE this BOOK!

Don't let the impact of this book end with you!
Get a discount
when you order
3 or MORE BOOKS.
CALL 1-888-987-7033

AUTHOR INTERVIEWS

Exclusive interviews with your favorite authors!
Tune in today.
voiceofdestiny.net

Destiny Image is a division of Nori Media Group.

Made in the USA
Coppell, TX
31 May 2021